ORTHO
Flower
PROBLEM SOLVER

...dith® Books
...Moines, Iowa

Flower Problem Solver

Editor: Denny Schrock
Contributing Editor: Kate Carter Frederick
Contributing Technical Editor: Michael D. Smith
Contributing Writer: Lynn Steiner
Copy Chief: Terri Fredrickson
Publishing Operations Manager: Karen Schirm
Senior Editor, Asset and Information Manager:
 Phillip Morgan
Edit and Design Production Coordinator: Mary Lee Gavin
Editorial Assistant: Kathleen Stevens
Book Production Managers: Pam Kvitne,
 Marjorie J. Schenkelberg, Rick von Holdt, Mark Weaver
Contributing Copy Editor: Kelly Roberson
Technical Proofreader: B. Rosie Lerner
Contributing Proofreaders: Becky Etchen, Jodie Littleton,
 Wendy Pohlemus-Annibel
Contributing Map Illustrator: Jana Fothergill
Contributing Photo Researcher: Susan Ferguson
Indexer: Ellen Sherron
Other Contributors: Janet Anderson, Irene Swartz

Additional Editorial Contributions from Art Rep Services
Director: Chip Nadeau
Designer: lk Design

Meredith® Books
Executive Director, Editorial: Gregory H. Kayko
Executive Director, Design: Matt Strelecki
Managing Editor: Amy Tincher-Durik
Executive Editor/Group Manager: Benjamin W. Allen
Senior Associate Design Director: Tom Wegner
Marketing Product Manager: Isaac Petersen

Publisher and Editor in Chief: James D. Blume
Editorial Director: Linda Raglan Cunningham
Executive Director, New Business Development:
 Todd M. Davis
Executive Director, Sales: Ken Zagor
Director, Operations: George A. Susral
Director, Production: Douglas M. Johnston
Director, Marketing: Amy Nichols
Business Director: Jim Leonard

Vice President and General Manager: Douglas J. Guendel

Meredith Publishing Group
President: Jack Griffin
Executive Vice President: Bob Mate

Meredith Corporation
Chairman and Chief Executive Officer: William T. Kerr
President and Chief Operating Officer: Stephen M. Lacy

In Memoriam: E.T. Meredith III (1933–2003)

Note to the Readers: Due to differing conditions, tools, and individual skills, Meredith Corporation assumes no responsibility for any damages, injuries suffered, or losses incurred as a result of following the information published in this book. Before beginning any project, review the instructions carefully, and if any doubts or questions remain, consult local experts or authorities. Because codes and regulations vary greatly, you always should check with authorities to ensure that your project complies with all applicable local codes and regulations. Always read and observe all of the safety precautions provided by manufacturers of any tools, equipment, or supplies, and follow all accepted safety procedures.

Photographers
(Photographers credited may retain copyright © to the photographs listed.)
L=Left, R=Right
Liz Ball/Positive Images: 67R;
Patricia Bruno/Positive Images: 23R, 34L, 40R; **William T. Crow:** 38 R; **Derek Fell:** 22L, 35R, 44R, 46R, 48L, 69R; **Margaret Hensel/Positive Images:** 64R; **Jerry Howard/Positive Images:** 10; **Bill Johnson:** 47R, 70L, 70R, 80L, 87L, 89R; **Gary Moorman:** 92L, 92R; **Leanne Pundt:** 33R; **Michael Thompson:** 39R, 41L, 67L, 74L, 74R, 88L; **Mike Wilkins:** 71R.

All of us at Meredith® Books are dedicated to providing you with the information and ideas you need to enhance your home and garden. We welcome your comments and suggestions about this book. Write to us at:
 Meredith Corporation
 Meredith Gardening Books
 1716 Locust St.
 Des Moines, IA 50309–3023

If you would like more information on other Ortho products, call 800/225-2883 or visit us at: www.ortho.com

Contents

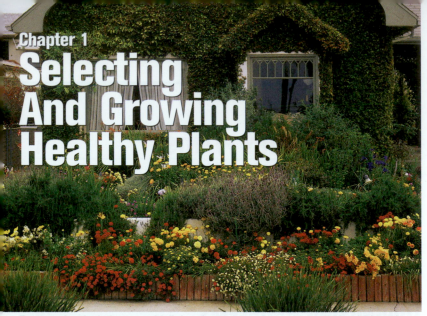

Chapter 1
Selecting And Growing Healthy Plants

Flowers perform best when you match their environmental requirements for sunlight, moisture, and fertility to the conditions in your garden.

Flowers can turn a drab yard into a showplace. Home gardeners turn to annuals, perennials, biennials, and bulbs to provide season-long color. Each type of plant requires a different approach in terms of planning, planting, and care.

Choosing flowers

There are several factors to keep in mind when choosing flowers, including hardiness, sunlight, drainage, and fertilizer requirements as well as flower color and bloom time. You should also choose your flowers based on how you will use them. Certain flowers are better than others for cutting, and annuals generally do better in containers than perennials or bulbs. If you are planting a large area,

you'll probably want to go with perennials so you don't have to replant each year.

While annuals and most biennials can be grown in most climates, hardiness must be considered for perennials and bulbs. Hardiness ratings based on minimum winter temperatures correspond to the USDA Plant Hardiness Zone map on page 5.

Annuals naturally live and die in a year or less. They are good for providing season-long color, but they must be replanted every year in cold climates. Gardeners living in areas with light or no frosts can plant a series of annuals to provide color almost all year long.

Perennials are non-woody plants that survive for many years when grown properly. They bloom for a limited time each year; this can be a

week or a month. Many offer interesting foliage when they are not in bloom. Some perennials completely die back and disappear after flowering, then emerge again the following year.

Biennial plants start their life cycle one year, go dormant in winter, then bloom and complete their lives the following year. If you want blooming biennials on a continual basis, you need to plant some new ones each year.

Bulbs are plants that grow from underground storage structures, including true bulbs, corms, tubers, rhizomes, and tuberous roots. Many are planted in fall for spring bloom, but some are planted in spring to bloom in summer. Once planted, they remain in place, often multiplying to produce more plants.

USDA PLANT HARDINESS ZONE MAP

This map of climate zones helps you select plants for your garden that will survive a typical winter in your region. The United States Department of Agriculture (USDA) developed the map, basing the zones on the average recorded low temperatures across North America. Zone 1 is the coldest area and Zone 11 is the warmest.

Plants are classified by the coldest temperature and zone they can endure. For example, plants hardy to Zone 6 survive where winter temperatures drop to –10°F. Those hardy to Zone 8 die long before it's that cold. These plants may grow in colder regions but must be replaced each year. Plants rated for a range of

hardiness zones can usually survive winter in the coldest region as well as tolerate the summer heat of the warmest one.

To find your hardiness zone, note the approximate location of your community on the map, then match the color band marking that area to the key.

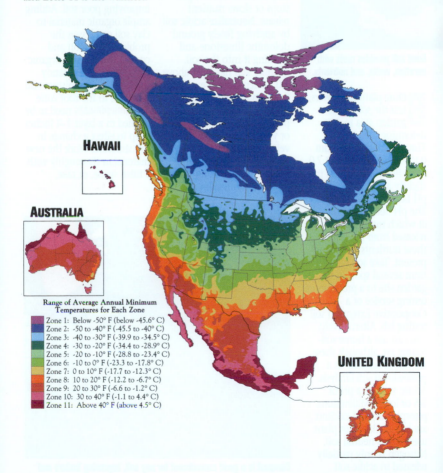

HAWAII

AUSTRALIA

UNITED KINGDOM

Range of Average Annual Minimum Temperatures for Each Zone

- Zone 1: Below -50° F (below -45.6° C)
- Zone 2: -50 to -40° F (-45.5 to -40° C)
- Zone 3: -40 to -30° F (-39.9 to -34.5° C)
- Zone 4: -30 to -20° F (-34.4 to -28.9° C)
- Zone 5: -20 to -10° F (-28.8 to -23.4° C)
- Zone 6: -10 to 0° F (-23.3 to -17.8° C)
- Zone 7: 0 to 10° F (-17.7 to -12.3° C)
- Zone 8: 10 to 20° F (-12.2 to -6.7° C)
- Zone 9: 20 to 30° F (-6.6 to -1.2° C)
- Zone 10: 30 to 40° F (-1.1 to 4.4° C)
- Zone 11: Above 40° F (above 4.5° C)

Soil pH and Soil Amendments

Good soil provides roots with aeration, water, and nutrients.

Before planting flowers, test the soil in the garden area to determine the pH level. The pH scale ranges from 0 to 14, with neutral at 7.0. Most flowers grow best in a slightly acidic soil with a pH between 6.5 and 7.0. The pH determines the rate at which nutrients are released from the soil, if these nutrients are already present. Take soil samples from several spots in the garden site to a professional testing service or a Cooperative Extension soil testing lab. Alternatively, you can use a home soil-testing kit, although these are not as accurate as a professional soil analysis. **Acidic soil** has a pH of 5.5 or lower. Magnesium, phosphorus, and calcium are less available for plant use than in neutral soil. Nitrogen is only partially released in acidic soil because the soil organisms that free it are less active. When soil has a pH of 5.0 or lower, soil organisms cease working altogether and no nitrogen is released.

Flowers in overly acidic soil may grow slowly, leaves may be pale, and root development may be poor. Overly acidic soil promotes disease mechanisms. Applying fertilizer may not help because the low pH stops or slows nutrient release. Neutralize acidic soil by applying finely ground dolomitic limestone and working it into the soil. **Alkaline soil** has a pH above 7.0. When the pH exceeds 8.0, iron and manganese are no longer available to the plants. Leaves become pale or yellow between their veins. To correct mildly alkaline soil, apply acidic peat moss, elemental sulfur, or ammonium sulfate.

Using a fertilizer for acid-loving plants also helps lower pH. If the soil pH is very high, you may need to plant flowers in raised beds filled with a commercial soil mix.

For flowers to thrive, you must improve poor soil. Organic amendments such as peat moss, compost, well-rotted manure, ground bark, and sawdust are best for improving poor soil. Adding ample organic material to clay soil can lessen the problems of runoff and compaction. Ample organic matter mixed into sandy soil helps hold moisture and nutrients in the root zone. **Soil amendments** need to be applied in a layer 1–4 inches deep to effect a change in soil structure. Work the new material in thoroughly with a tiller, spade, or rake.

Compost is a good amendment for any soil, improving texture and adding nutrients.

GROWING ANNUALS

Impatiens are an excellent choice for season-long color in the shade.

Many annuals, including cosmos, respond to deadheading by producing more blooms.

Most annuals need full sun for at least 4–6 hours a day to flower well, but some, such as impatiens, coleus, and begonias, are shade tolerant.

Annuals can be direct-seeded in prepared beds, started indoors for transplanting outside later, or purchased as ready-to-plant transplants. Most summer annuals can be seeded indoors 6–8 weeks before the last spring frost. Wait to plant tender annuals outdoors until the danger of frost has passed. Many flowering annuals, even if not injured by low temperatures, will not grow well until the soil warms. Plant winter annuals at least 6 weeks before the expected first fall frost date to allow time for root development.

Plant annuals with the top of the roots just under the surface of the soil. Be sure to remove paper, fiber, and plastic pots before planting. Remove the upper edges of peat pots so that the pot will not act as a wick, pulling water away from the roots. Pinch off any buds and flowers when planting to promote better branching structure and a stronger plant.

Pay especially close attention to watering the first few weeks. Most annuals need at least 1–1½ inches of water per week from rain or irrigation. More may be needed during very hot weather. To promote deep root growth, water thoroughly and deeply. Allow the soil surface to dry before watering again. Soaker hoses and drip irrigation are ideal watering methods since they save water and avoid wetting leaves and flowers.

Mulch flowerbeds with 2–3 inches of shredded leaves, pine bark, or pine straw to help conserve soil moisture and reduce weed growth.

Annual plants usually require additional fertilizer during the growing season. Water-soluble fertilizers give fast, but temporary, effects. Slow-release fertilizers are expensive but convenient and easy to apply.

As flowers fade, remove them before seeds are formed to keep plants looking attractive and to encourage continuing flowering. Pruning can invigorate some species. Petunias can be cut back in midsummer to within a few inches of the ground, fertilized, and heavily watered, and they will be full and attractive again in just a few weeks.

Flowering annuals vary in their insect and disease susceptibility. Choose insect- and disease-resistant species and cultivars when possible. Keep the garden clean and weed-free, and be alert for early signs of trouble to reduce the need for pesticides. To prevent the spread of leaf diseases, avoid overhead watering if possible and water early in the morning to allow the plants to dry quickly. Overwatering can lead to root decay.

The most common insect pests are aphids, spider mites, whiteflies, and caterpillars. Infestations are more easily controlled early, before the population has a chance to expand.

GROWING PERENNIALS AND BIENNIALS

Perennials bloom for a limited time each year, but make up for it by living longer in the garden.

All newly planted flowers should be watered well. Mulching helps conserve water and reduce weeds.

There are perennials and biennials for full sun or heavy shade, for dry or wet soil. Select plants suited to the growing conditions where they will be planted. Good air circulation helps avoid diseases.

Soil preparation is important for perennials, since they may be in place for many years. Spade the beds 8–10 inches deep, and work in at least 2 inches of compost or organic matter before planting.

Plant most perennials from spring to fall. Finish fall planting at least 6 weeks before hard freezes occur. In cold climates plant perennials in spring.

Perennials are available grown in containers, field-grown, or shipped bare-root and dormant. Some are easy to grow from seed. Water plants thoroughly following planting to settle the soil around the roots.

Pay close attention to watering the first few weeks while plants develop their root systems. Most require at least 1 inch of water per week from rain or irrigation. To promote deep root growth, water thoroughly and deeply. Allow the soil surface to dry before watering again. Soaker hoses and drip irrigation are ideal watering methods since they save water and avoid wetting leaves and flowers.

Mulch with a 1–2-inch layer of compost, shredded leaves, pine bark, or pine straw to help keep down weeds and conserve moisture. Avoid overly heavy mulching to help prevent crown rot. Weeds can be pulled by hand or controlled by a herbicide labeled for that flower.

Fertilization should be based on the results of a soil test. In the absence of a soil test, apply a complete fertilizer such as 8-8-8 or 10-10-10 at the rate of 1–2 pounds per 100 square feet of bed area just before new shoots emerge in early spring. Avoid touching any emerging leaves with the fertilizer to prevent leaf damage.

Many perennials should be staked to prevent them from bending or falling over during wind and rain. Remove old flowers to encourage rebloom. Many perennials should be cut back to ground level after bloom is finished to encourage new leaf growth from the base. Remove dead foliage and stems in the fall, and mulch to protect crowns and roots from alternating mild and freezing weather.

Most perennials eventually become overcrowded and require division. This can be done in spring or fall, depending on the individual plant.

Perennials vary considerably in their susceptibility to pests. Selection of resistant species and cultivars, proper site selection, and good cultural practices will prevent many disease problems.

GROWING BULBS

Spring-flowering bulbs grow best in sun or light shade. Some summer and fall bulbs grow well in sun, others in shade.

Good drainage is essential for all bulbs. Improve soil texture by mixing in 2–3 inches of organic matter. Raised beds can also help solve drainage problems.

The pH for most bulbs should be between 6 and 7. Fertilize bulbs by mixing a slow-release complete fertilizer or bonemeal mixed with fertilizer at the rate of 1–2 pounds of 10-10-10 per 100 square feet of garden bed at planting time.

Purchase spring bulbs during September or October. Large bulbs produce larger flowers. Choose firm bulbs without mold or bruising. Store bulbs below 60°F until planting. Plant summer-flowering bulbs in spring after frost danger is past. The soil temperature should be at least 55°F.

Plant bulbs 3–4 times as deep as the width of the bulb. Space large bulbs 3–6 inches apart, small bulbs 1–2 inches. For best appearance, plant bulbs in masses. Cover the bed with 2–3 inches of mulch after planting.

If conditions are hot or dry during spring bloom, additional water will help prolong flowering. Summer- and fall-flowering bulbs need plenty of water while actively growing.

Remove the flowers of tulips and daffodils after they fade to prevent seed formation. Leave foliage on the plant for at least 6 weeks after bloom or until it turns brown. This allows the leaves to build up the bulb for next year's bloom.

Many bulbs eventually become overcrowded and must be divided and replanted. Dig bulbs after the foliage has turned yellow and withered. Replant divided bulbs immediately or store in a dry, cool area for fall replanting. Discard any bulbs that appear diseased. Some tender summer-flowering bulbs, such as caladiums and tuberous begonias, should be harvested and stored before the first fall frost. Allow the bulbs to air-dry for 1–2 days and store them in a cool, dry place until spring planting.

Protect bulbs from animals by enclosing the bulbs in ½-inch wire mesh baskets or line planting beds with mesh before planting. Aphids and thrips may cause young leaves to show puckering, curling, or other abnormalities. Viruses can occur in all bulbs. Variegation may occur in the flower, yellow streaks may develop in the leaves, and plants are generally smaller and weaker. Destroy all infected plants as they appear, and control all sucking insects that can transmit viruses.

Spring-blooming bulbs need to be planted in fall, while they are dormant.

Planting bulbs in a wire mesh basket will keep them safe from hungry gophers.

Careful examination of your affected flower is important for accurate diagnosis of problems.

Chapter 2
Diagnosing Problems

Ortho's *Flower Problem Solver* is designed to help you diagnose a flower problem and provide potential solutions. The key to accurate diagnosis is knowing how to look for clues to a problem and what types of clues to look for. The checklist on page 11 gives a step-by-step procedure for gathering clues and diagnosing a problem. It will help you develop a case history, eliminate unlikely sources of the problem, and find the real cause.

How to observe

Begin your observations by examining your plant. Note its general conditions. Is the entire plant affected or only select areas? A 5- to 15-power hand lens will allow you to see insects or symptoms not easily visible to the naked eye. The key to many plant problems is in the soil. Investigate the drainage, probe the soil with an auger to determine the depth and type, or test the pH of the soil.

If the initial inspection does not reveal any obvious reason for the symptoms, developing a case history for the plant may lead you to a less conspicuous cause of the problem. Some problems are more prevalent at certain times of the year.

Putting it all together

After studying your ailing plant, look through the general problem headings at the tops of the pages in the problem-solution section. Find the heading that applies to your problem, then see if one of the descriptions fits your problem. Read carefully. Every word and phrase is important for understanding the nature of the problem. "May" means that the symptom develops only sometimes. And certain phrases offer you clues about the problem, such as the time of year to expect it and where to look for the symptoms.

Unfortunately, flowers frequently develop more than one problem at a time.

Plants have natural defenses against diseases and insects. But when one problem weakens a plant, and lowers its defenses, other problems are able to infect it. For uncommon problems, you may want to refer to *The Ortho Problem Solver*— a professional edition found at many nurseries and in garden and home-improvement centers.

Once you have determined what the problem is, decide on a treatment. Not all problems require treatment, and not all problems require treatment all of the time. Many insect problems are purely cosmetic and don't necessarily affect the overall health of the plant. Many disease problems are most effectively treated with preventative fungicides; spraying after symptoms are seen is often ineffective. You should decide what your level of tolerance is before deciding on a treatment.

In some cases it may not be possible for an untrained homeowner to accurately diagnose a problem. If you've studied the sick plant carefully, gone through the checklist, and still can't be sure of the problem, seek the help of a professional, especially if the solution involves the use of chemical control.

CHECKLIST FOR DIAGNOSIS

Use this checklist to develop a case history for the problem and to identify symptoms that will lead to an accurate diagnosis.

WHAT TO LOOK FOR

Plant characteristics

■ What type of flower is it and when was it established?

■ Does it prefer moist or dry conditions?

■ Does it prefer cold or warmth?

■ Does it grow best in acid or alkaline soil?

■ Is the plant young and tender, or is it old and in a state of decline?

■ Is the plant abnormally small?

Location of plant

■ Was the plant recently transplanted?

■ Has it had time to become established, or are all its roots still in the original root ball?

■ Is the property located downwind from a factory, or is it in a large polluted urban area?

■ Is the plant next to a building? If so, is the location sunny or shady? How intense is the reflected light?

■ How close is the plant to a road? Is salt used to deice the road in the winter?

■ Are there large shade trees overhead?

■ Are nearby plants also affected? Do the same species show similar symptoms? Are unrelated plants affected? How close are other affected plants?

Symptom development

■ When were the symptoms first noticed?

■ Have symptoms been developing for a long time, or did they appear suddenly?

Condition of plant

■ Is the entire planting affected, or is the problem found only on one plant?

■ What parts of the plant are affected?

■ Are the leaves abnormal in size, color, shape, or texture?

■ Do the flowers show symptoms?

■ What do the roots look like? Are they white and healthy, or are they discolored?

■ Do you see any insects, or is there evidence of insects, such as holes in the leaves or chewed roots?

■ Has the problem appeared in past years?

Weather and sunlight

■ Have weather conditions been unusual (cold, hot, dry, wet, windy, snowy, and so on) recently or during the past few years?

■ How much light does the plant receive? Is it the optimum amount for this flower?

■ Is the plant growing under something that blocks rainfall or sprinkler water?

■ How windy is the location?

Soil conditions

■ What kind of soil is the plant growing in? Is it predominantly clay, sand, or loam?

■ How deep is the soil? Is a layer of rock or hardpan beneath the topsoil?

■ What is the soil pH?

■ Does the soil drain well? Does the soil have a sour smell?

■ Is the soil compacted?

■ Has the soil been mulched or covered with crushed rock?

■ Was the mulch obtained from a reputable dealer?

■ Are weeds or grass growing around the base of the plant? How thickly?

Recent care

■ Has the plant or surrounding gardens been fertilized or watered recently?

■ If fertilizer was used, was it applied according to label directions?

■ Has the plant been treated with herbicide, fungicide, or insecticide?

■ Was the treatment for this problem or another one?

■ Was the pesticide registered for use on this plant?

■ Was the pesticide applied according to label directions?

■ Did rain wash off the spray immediately after it was applied?

■ Did you repeat the spray if the label suggested it?

■ Have weed killers or lawn weed-and-feed fertilizer been used in the area in the past year? How close?

■ Did you spray on a windy day?

WEEDS, DISEASES, AND FLOWER PESTS

Weeds

The best approach to weed control is a good defense. Eliminate as many weeds as possible before planting. Use mulch to prevent weed seeds from germinating and to smother weeds.

If you can't control weeds through cultural practices, you may need to resort to chemical control. Herbicides are generally grouped into two categories: preemergent and postemergent. A preemergent stops sprouting at an early stage and is most effective when applied before weed seeds germinate. A postemergent control is effective after the weeds have emerged and begun to grow.

Read the herbicide label carefully before purchasing and using the product. Make sure the chemical is appropriate for the plant you want to treat, and see if using the product requires special precautions. Use all controls at the appropriate time. Avoid spraying or dusting on windy days. Wind can waft weed killers to nearby plants. Apply chemical controls early in the morning or at dusk, when the air is generally calm. If the herbicide label does not list a nearby plant as safe for the product, protect the plant with a cardboard or wood barrier when spraying.

A treatment can take 3–10 days to produce visible results. Do not reapply the product if weed browning does not occur a day or two after spraying. Herbicide overdoses are dangerous to surrounding plants. Weed killers do not gain effectiveness if mixed at a concentration stronger than the instructions recommend. Using too strong a mixture can damage or kill desirable garden plants.

Wash all applicators thoroughly with water and detergent to remove traces of herbicides. Better yet, use separate applicators for herbicides, fungicides, and insecticides.

Diseases

Most diseases are caused by fungi or bacteria that thrive in moist conditions. They can be spread by wind or

Mulch reduces weeds, conserves water, and keeps flowers cleaner.

Whenever possible, examine the roots of affected plants. Many problems start there.

Ladybugs are among the beneficial insects that prey on aphids.

Hover flies are beneficial insects that resemble bees and wasps.

splashing water or live in the soil. To reduce chances of infection, do all you can to keep the leaves dry. Water in the early morning so plants have time to dry off well before cooler evening temperatures set in. To reduce infection from soil-borne diseases, improve drainage and water less frequently so the soil has a chance to dry out between watering cycles.

A healthy plant is the best defense against disease problems. Choose a plant based on your site and climate, improve soil conditions if necessary, and water, fertilize, and prune as necessary.

Most fungicides provide a protective barrier on the leaf surface. To be effective, they must be applied before the spore lands on the leaf, so timing is important with fungicidal sprays. The fungicide must also be renewed periodically as it wears off. Once symptoms

are well developed, it's usually too late to spray for the current season. The following spring, treat with an appropriate fungicide before symptoms appear. Always read the label carefully before applying any chemical controls.

Flower pests

Pests are usually grouped into two categories: insects and larger animals.

Insect pests can invade in small or large numbers. Healthy plants can tolerate more insect damage than poorly maintained plants. Large populations of any pest insect species usually call for intervention by the gardener. Biological controls—such as birds, parasitic wasps, *Bacillus thuringiensis* (Bt), ladybugs, and green lacewing larvae— can help control insect pests. It is important to identify the pest and its damage before deciding

on any chemical control. Always read the label carefully before applying any chemical controls.

A problem with using insecticides is that they often harm beneficial insects such as ladybugs, praying mantis, hover flies, lacewings, and parasitic wasps. Use insecticides appropriately and read the label carefully before spraying to avoid harming insects that are beneficial natural predators.

Deer, moles, rabbits, and gophers top the list of animal pests, although in certain areas birds, armadillos, skunks, voles (also called meadow mice or field mice), can cause significant damage. Control methods include trapping, baits, repellents, installation of barriers, and removal of food sources. For more information on controlling animal pests, *see page 84.*

Chapter 3
Flower Problems

How to use this book

The photographs at the top of the pages are arranged so that similar symptoms are grouped together. Select the picture that looks most like your problem.

The solution section of each problem assumes that you have seen the problem at the time when the symptoms first become obvious. Each solution begins by telling you what you can do immediately to alleviate the problem. Then it tells you what changes you can make in the growing environment or in your flower-care practices to prevent the problem from recurring.

When Ortho has products to treat a problem, the products are identified by name. If Ortho does not make a product to solve a particular problem, generic chemical solutions listed by the common name of the active ingredient are included. When an Ortho product is listed, it will do the job for which it is recommended, and it will not harm your plant if you use it according to label directions. Be sure that the plant you wish to spray is listed on the product label. Always read pesticide labels carefully and follow label directions to the letter.

Group of similar symptoms

A photograph depicting a typical symptom or organism

The problem name

The problem section describes the symptom or symptoms.

The analysis section describes the organisms or cultural conditions causing the problem, including life cycles, natural processes, typical progress of the problem, and its seriousness.

POOR FLOWERING (continued)
Few or no flowers on bulbs

Undersized tulip bulbs blooming poorly.

Planting large, healthy tulip bulbs deeply.

Problem: Narcissus and tulip bulbs produce healthy foliage (it may be sparse) but few or no flowers are produced. Flowers that are produced may be smaller than normal.

Plants: Tulip and daffodil (Narcissus).

Analysis: 1. Overcrowding: Bulbs multiply each year, producing larger clumps the following spring.
2. Too much shade: Daffodils and tulips planted in shade usually bloom well the first year, but they require a sunny location for continued flowering over a long time.
3. Overheating: If bulbs are stored at warm temperatures (80°F and higher), the flower embryo inside the bulb is killed.
4. Undersized bulbs: If flower bulbs are smaller than normal, they may produce only foliage for the first 1–2 years.
5. Foliage removed too soon: If the foliage is removed before it has a chance to die back naturally, the new bulbs may not have enough food stored to produce a flower.
6. Lack of cooling: To flower properly, bulbs require a minimum of 15 weeks of cool temperatures (40–50°F).
7. Lack of nutrients to tulips: When tulips are grown in infertile soil for more than one season, they form small, poor-quality bulbs.
8. Old plantings of tulips: Tulip flowers are largest and most prolific the first spring after newly purchased bulbs have been planted. After flowering, several small "daughter bulbs" form. Often these daughter bulbs are too small to provide many flowers.

Solution: The numbered solutions below correspond to the numbered items in the analysis section above.
1. Divide bulbs every 3–4 years.
2. Grow daffodils and tulips in a location where they will receive 4 hours or more of full sun.
3. Store bulbs at cool temperatures (55–60°F) and in a well-ventilated location.
4. Purchase only large, healthy bulbs. Fertilize with Scotts® Bulb Slow Release Plant Food in fall and when shoots appear.
5. Let the foliage turn yellow before removing it.
6. In warm-weather areas (Zones 9 and 10; see page 5 for zone map), precool bulbs before planting, or buy precooled bulbs. Postpone planting until mid-December.
7. Add Scotts® Bulb Slow Release Plant Food when planting, when the new leaves appear in spring, and again after flowers bloom.
8. Replace old tulips with fresh bulbs. Prolong the flowering life of a tulip bed by planting the bulbs deeper than usual.

18 *Flower Problems*

A range map of the United States and southern Canada accompanies each problem. In areas that are red, the problem is severe or commonplace. In areas that are yellow, the problem is secondary or occasional. In areas that are white, the problem is rare or nonexistent.

The plants section lists flowers that are especially susceptible to this problem.

The solution section provides short-term and long-term techniques to mitigate or cure the problem.

POOR FLOWERING
Transplant shock

Transplant shock on cineraria.

Transplanting rudbeckia.

Problem: Recently transplanted flowers drop their flower buds before they open. Often, blossoms and leaves also drop prematurely. The plant may wilt during the hot part of the day even if the soil is moist.

Plants: All annuals, perennials, and biennials.

Analysis: Even under ideal conditions, many plants drop some of their buds, flowers, and leaves when transplanted. Bud and leaf drop result from root damage that occurs during transplanting. Tiny hairlike rootlets that grow at the periphery of the root system absorb most of the water the plant uses. When these rootlets are damaged during transplanting, the amount of water that can be supplied to the foliage and flowers is decreased. Flower buds, flowers, and leaves fall off, and the plant wilts. The more the roots are damaged during transplanting, the greater will be the leaf and bud drop. Also, because plants lose water rapidly during hot, dry, windy periods, transplanting at these times will cause plants to undergo greater shock. They will not recover as quickly. As the root system regrows, new flower buds will form.

Solution: Transplant when the weather is cool, in the early morning, in the late afternoon, and on cloudy days. Whenever possible, transplant small plants rather than large ones. When transplanting, disturb the soil around the roots as little as possible. Preserve as much of the root system as possible. If the roots have been disturbed, or if the plant is large or old, pinch off about one-third of the growth to reduce the amount of foliage needing water.

Few or no flowers

Poor flowering on gazania.

Deadheading coreopsis to promote rebloom.

Problem: There are few blooms, and the flowers may be smaller than normal.

Plants: All annuals, perennials, and biennials may be affected.

Analysis: Lack of flowers can result from any of several causes, including both pathological (disease) and nonpathological problems.

1. Insufficient light: Many plants require full- or part-day sun to flower properly. Even plants that flower well in filtered light will not produce as many blossoms when planted in deep shade. Plants receiving inadequate light are often leggy or spindly.

2. Diseased plants: Plants that have been attacked by disease or insect pests rarely flower well. Mottled, discolored, or dying foliage or chewed leaves usually indicate the presence of a disease organism or insect pest.

3. Old flowers left on plant: Many plants slow down their flower production when the older blossoms are allowed to fade and form seeds. The plant diverts its energy into producing seeds rather than flowers.

4. Overcrowding: Plants that are overcrowded must compete for light, nutrients, and water. When supplies of nutrients are inadequate, overall plant growth, including flowering, decreases.

5. Too much nitrogen: Plants require a balanced diet of nutrients (nitrogen, phosphorous, and potassium) to grow and bloom properly. Excessive nitrogen from high-nitrogen fertilizers throws off the balance on nutrients and encourages lush, green leaf growth at the expense of flower production.

Small blossoms on petunia.

Dividing moss phlox to reduce overcrowding.

Solution: The numbered solutions below correspond to the numbered items in the analysis section at left.

1. Use a reliable reference to check the light requirements of your plants. Most flowering plants are full-sun plants, which means they need a minimum of 6 hours of sun a day. If plants are not receiving enough light, move them to a sunnier location and replace them with plants that can tolerate some shade. For shade-tolerant plants, it is important to understand the different degrees of shade, which can range from light to heavy and are different at different times of the growing season. "Light shade" areas receive bright light or some sun for all but a few hours each day. Areas with bright light or sun for about half the day are called "partial shade." Most shade plants will do fine in either of these sites, especially if the sun is morning sun. If you want to grow flowering plants in the shade of large trees, if may be necessary to limb up some taller trees to allow more sunlight to reach the ground.

2. Look up your plant in the index to see what diseases and insects may affect it, and treat accordingly. Be sure to accurately diagnose a disease problem so you can choose the best method of control. If your plant repeatedly suffers from the same disease or insect problem year after year, you should consider replacing it with a plant that is better adapted to the conditions.

3. Remove flowers as they start to fade to prevent them from forming seeds. This process is called "deadheading." It is especially effective in prolonging the bloom of annual plants, but it can also extend the bloom time of some perennials. To be effective, you must remove the entire flowering structure, not just the petals. If you want your plants to reseed the following year, stop deadheading toward the end of the summer to allow some plants to set seed.

4. Thin overcrowded plantings of perennials. Most perennials do best if they are divided every 3–5 years. Division is best done in the cool, moist days of early spring and early fall. If you must divide in the heat of summer, try to do it on a cloudy day, water the newly planted divisions well, and provide some type of shade for the first week or so after dividing.

5. Fertilize your plants with Miracle-Gro® Bloom Booster or a fertilizer with a high middle number (phosphorous) and low first number (nitrogen). The extra phosphate in the fertilizer helps to promote flowering.

Few or no flowers on bulbs

Undersized tulip bulbs blooming poorly.

Planting large, healthy tulip bulbs deeply.

Problem: Narcissus and tulip bulbs produce healthy foliage (it may be sparse) but few or no flowers are produced. Flowers that are produced may be smaller than normal.

Plants: Tulip and daffodil *(Narcissus).*

Analysis: 1. Overcrowding: Bulbs multiply each year, producing larger clumps the following spring.
2. Too much shade: Daffodils and tulips planted in shade usually bloom well the first year, but they require a sunny location for continued flowering over a long time.
3. Overheating: If bulbs are stored at warm temperatures (80°F and higher), the flower embryo inside the bulb is killed.
4. Undersized bulbs: If flower bulbs are smaller than normal, they may produce only foliage for the first 1–2 years.
5. Foliage removed too soon: If the foliage is removed before it has a chance to die back naturally, the new bulbs may not have enough food stored to produce a flower.
6. Lack of cooling: To flower properly, bulbs require a minimum of 15 weeks of cool temperatures (40–50°F).
7. Lack of nutrients to tulips: When tulips are grown in infertile soil for more than one season, they form small, poor-quality bulbs.
8. Old plantings of tulips: Tulip flowers are largest and most prolific the first spring after newly purchased bulbs have been planted. After flowering, several small "daughter bulbs" form. Often these daughter bulbs are too small to provide many flowers.

Solution: The numbered solutions below correspond to the numbered items in the analysis section above.
1. Divide bulbs every 3–4 years.
2. Grow daffodils and tulips in a location where they will receive 4 hours or more of full sun.
3. Store bulbs at cool temperatures (55–60°F) and in a well-ventilated location.
4. Purchase only large, healthy bulbs. Fertilize with Scotts® Bulb Slow Release Plant Food in fall and when shoots appear.
5. Let the foliage turn yellow before removing it.
6. In warm-weather areas (Zones 9 and 10; *see page 5* for zone map), precool bulbs before planting, or buy precooled bulbs. Postpone planting until mid-December.
7. Add Scotts® Bulb Slow Release Plant Food when planting, when the new leaves appear in spring, and again after flowers bloom.
8. Replace old tulips with fresh bulbs. Prolong the flowering life of a tulip bed by planting the bulbs deeper than usual.

Few or no flowers on peony

Bud blast on peony.

Foliage but no bloom on peony.

Problem: Peonies fail to produce flower buds, or they produce buds that fail to develop fully. Buds may turn black or brown and eventually dry up.

Plants: Peony.

Analysis: Peonies may fail to bloom for several reasons.

1. Crown (where the stems meet the roots) buried at wrong depth: Peonies planted too deep or too shallow often fail to develop blooms.

2. Immature transplants: Peony roots that have been divided and transplanted usually fail to flower for at least 2 years. If the divisions were extremely small, the plants may not flower for as long as 5 years.

3. Crowded plantings: Old, established peony clumps eventually become overcrowded and stop producing flowers.

4. Too much shade: Peonies stop blooming when they are heavily shaded by trees, tall shrubs, or buildings.

5. Lack of fertilization: Peonies that are not fed enough fail to bloom.

6. Plants suffering from bud blast: Bud blast is a disease that was previously blamed on gray mold, but the cause is usually cultural. Any factor not conducive to healthy growth is a possible cause. These factors include dry spells, lack of potassium, low temperatures during early spring, overly deep planting, excessive root competition or shade, infertile soil, and root infestation by nematodes.

Solution: The numbered solutions below correspond to the numbered items in the analysis section above.

1. Carefully dig up and reset the crown so that the eyes are 1½–2 inches below the soil surface.

2. With time, the young plants will mature and start flowering.

3. Peonies usually need to be divided after 6–10 years or anytime when flower production starts to drop off. Dig up and divide old clumps into divisions containing 3–5 eyes. These divisions may be replanted in the garden.

4. Transplant to a sunny location.

5. Apply Scotts® All Purpose Flower & Vegetable Slow Release Plant Food in early spring, and work it in lightly around each plant.

6. Supply ample sun and deep watering, and improve general growing conditions as needed, including those listed above. Do not cut plants back until foliage naturally turns brown in the fall.

Many small flowers

Small chrysanthemums without disbudding.

Disbudding a hybrid tea rose.

Problem: The plant produces many small flowers rather than a few large, showy flowers. The leaves are healthy.

Plants: Plants with large, showy flowers such as chrysanthemum, dahlia, peony, and carnation.

Analysis: Large, showy flowers will not be produced on certain plants, such as chrysanthemums, dahlias, and carnations, unless most of the flower buds are removed. Generally, these plants produce long stems with a terminal flower bud at the end and secondary flower buds at the base of each leaf. The plant has only a limited amount of nutrients with which to nourish each bud. If the plant has many buds, each flower bud will receive only a small amount of nutrients and will develop into a small bloom.

Solution: Pinch off the side flower buds as soon as they are large enough to be handled. The earlier they are removed, the larger the terminal flowers will be.

Flower thrips

Flower thrips damage to gladiolus.

Thrips damage to chrysanthemum.

Problem: Flower buds turn brown and die before they open. Silvery-white or brown streaks are often on the leaves. Flowers that have opened are often streaked and distorted. If the flower buds are peeled open, tiny (1/20-inch) insects resembling brown or straw-colored wood slivers can be seen moving around the base of the petals.

Plants: Many annuals, perennials, biennials, and bulbs; especially gladiolus.

Analysis: Several species of this common insect pest attack garden flowers. Thrips are found in protected parts of the plant, such as the insides of flower buds, where they feed by rasping the soft plant tissue, then sucking the released plant sap. The injured tissue dies and turns white or brown, causing the characteristic streaking of the leaves and flowers. Because thrips migrate long distances on wind currents, they can quickly infest widespread areas. In cold climates, thrips feed and reproduce from spring until fall. With the onset of freezing weather, they find sheltered areas and hibernate through the winter. In warm-weather climates, thrips feed and reproduce all year. These pests reach their population peak in late spring to midsummer. They are especially troublesome during prolonged dry spells.

Solution: Thrips can't be eliminated completely, but they can be kept under control. Spray infested plants with Ortho® Rose & Flower Insect Killer or Ortho® Systemic Insect Killer. Spray 2 or 3 times at intervals of 10 days as soon as damage is noticed. Make sure that your plant is listed on the product label. Repeat the spray if reinfestation occurs. Pick off and destroy old, infested flowers.

WILTING
Bacterial wilt

Aster showing symptoms of bacterial wilt.

Bacterial wilt on dianthus.

Problem: Stems and sometimes entire plants wilt. Leaves dry, turn yellow, and die. Roots are often rotted. Cracks may appear around the base of the stem, with yellow streaks extending up the length of the stem. When the stems are split open, yellowish to brownish discolorations of the stem tissue are revealed. The infected interior portions of the stem are sticky.

Plants: Many flowering plants, especially carnation and pinks (*Dianthus*).

Analysis: Several kinds of bacteria can cause bacterial wilt in flowers. Infection begins when bacteria in the soil or on contaminated tools and hands penetrate wounds in the roots, leaves, or stems or when infested seed is planted. In some cases, infection begins when insects transmit the bacteria to healthy plants. The bacteria enter the water-conducting vessels of the plants, where they break down plant cells, producing gums and gels. The bacteria slowly move out of these vessels to attach and dissolve the walls of adjacent cells. Sometimes bacterial ooze emerges from cracks in the leaf and stem tissue. The accumulation of gels, gums, cell debris, and bacteria in the vessel clogs the water flow throughout the plant. This closing and the destruction of cell walls cause the plant to discolor, wilt, and finally die. Bacterial wilt increases as the temperature grows warmer.

Solution: Once a plant is infected, it can't be cured. It is best to remove and destroy all infected plants. Clean up plant debris. If you've been handling infected plants, wash your hands thoroughly with soap and hot water, and disinfect any contaminated tools. Don't replant healthy carnations or pinks in contaminated soil. Avoid damage to plants when cultivating.

Black stem rot

Black stem rot symptoms on geranium stems.

Foliar symptoms of geranium with black stem rot.

Problem: Dark lesions form at the base of the stems. These lesions enlarge and turn black and shiny. The blackening progresses up the stem. The leaves wilt and drop, and the plant may eventually die.

Plants: Many flowering plants, especially annual geranium (*Pelargonium*).

Analysis: Black stem rot is a common disease of geraniums caused by a fungus (*Pythium* species) that lives in the soil. It thrives in wet, poorly drained soil. The fungus attacks the stems at the soil level, then spreads upward. Stems decay and the foliage wilts, shrivels, and eventually dies. Black stem rot spreads through contaminated soil, transplants, and tools.

Solution: Remove and destroy infected plants. If they have been growing in containers, throw out the soil in which they grew. Wash and disinfect contaminated tools and pots. Plant healthy geraniums in well-drained soil and let them dry out between waterings. If the geraniums are in containers, you can try this drying-out technique. Stop watering infected plants. To dry the soil as quickly as possible, place the containers in a well-ventilated, even breezy location in full sun. But if the roots are damaged badly enough that plants wilt or drop leaves, don't put them in the sun. Eventually the soil will dry out to the point where the plants would normally need another watering. Allow the soil to become drier still to stop the fungi from continuing their decay. Take steps to minimize the water needs of the plants, such as by placing the container in the shade. Begin watering again when the plant shows signs of drought stress, such as heavy wilting or yellowing and dropping of leaves.

Fusarium wilt

Fusarium wilt on dianthus.

Healthy flowers and foliage of dianthus.

Problem: Leaves and stems turn gray-green, then pale yellow, and then wilt. Yellowing and wilting often affect only one side of the plant. Plant shoots may be curled and distorted. Stems are soft and can easily be crushed. When a stem is split open, dark streaks and discoloration of the inner water-conducting stem tissue are revealed. The roots generally appear healthy.

Plants: Many flowering plants.

Analysis: Fusarium wilt disease affects many ornamental plants. It is caused by a soil-inhabiting fungus *(Fusarium)* that persists indefinitely on plant debris or in the soil. The disease spreads through contaminated seeds, plants, soil, and equipment. The fungus enters the plant through the roots and spreads up into the stems and leaves through water-conducting vessels in the stems. The vessels become discolored and plugged. This plugging cuts off the flow of water to the leaves, causing leaf yellowing and wilting. *See also* Fusarium Yellows *on page 58.*

Solution: No chemical control is available. It is best to destroy infected plants. Fusarium can be removed from the soil only by fumigation or solarization techniques. The best solution is to use plants that are resistant to fusarium.

Heat or acute root damage

Transplanting cranesbill, perennial geranium.

Wilt from transplant shock on ligularia.

Problem: The plant is wilting, but the foliage looks healthy. No signs of disease or insects are present. The soil is moist.

Plants: All annuals, perennials, biennials, and bulbs.

Analysis: If a plant wilts in moist soil but the leaves look healthy, one of the following situations has probably occurred recently.

1. Intense heat or wind: During hot, windy periods, plants may wilt even though the soil is wet. Wind and heat cause water to evaporate quickly from the leaves. The roots can't take in water as fast as it is lost.

2. Transplant shock: Plants frequently wilt soon after being transplanted as a result of injured roots. Roots are usually broken or injured to some degree during transplanting. Damaged roots are unable to supply the plant with enough water, even when the soil is wet. As the root system restores itself, its water-absorbing capacity increases. Unless they are severely injured, plants will soon recover.

3. Rodents: Bulbs or roots of plants are gnawed. Plants may be pushed up out of the ground.

4. Mechanical injury: Cultivating, digging, hoeing, thinning, weeding, and any other kind of activity that damages plant roots or stems can cause wilting.

Solution: Solutions below correspond to the numbered items in the analysis above.

1. As long as the soil is kept moist during periods of intense heat and wind, the plants will probably recover without harm when the temperature drops or the wind dies. Shading the plants and sprinkling them with water to cool off the foliage and reduce the rate of water evaporation from the leaves may hasten recovery.

2. Preserve the root system as much as possible when transplanting. Keep as much of the soil around the roots as possible. Transplant when the weather is cool, in the early morning, late afternoon, or on cloudy days. If the roots have been disturbed, or if the plant is large and old, prune about one-third of the growth. If possible, transplant when the plant is dormant.

3. Rodents may be trapped or baited. Install a barrier around bulbs at planting.

4. Prevent mechanical injury to plants by working very carefully around them. Cultivate as shallowly as possible.

Lack of water

Leaf-edge damage to hosta caused by wilting.

Astilbe requires ample moisture. Water it often.

Problem: The plant wilts often, and the soil is frequently or always dry. The leaves turn brown, shrivel, and may be crisp.

Plants: All annuals, perennials, biennials, and bulbs.

Analysis: The most common cause of plant wilting is dry soil. Plant roots transport water up into the stems and leaves, and it evaporates into the air through microscopic breathing pores in the surface of the leaves. Water pressure in the plant cells keeps the cell walls rigid and prevents the plant from collapsing. When the soil is dry, the roots are unable to furnish the leaves and stems with water, the water pressure in the cells drops, and the plant wilts. Most plants will recover if they have not wilted severely. Frequent or severe wilting, however, will curb a plant's growth and eventually kill it.

Solution: Water the plant thoroughly, applying enough water to wet the soil to the bottom of the root zone. Soils vary greatly in their ability to hold water. To see how much water your soil needs to wet it a foot deep, measure the amount of water you apply during watering. The next day, after the water has moved down as far as it will go (clay soils may take 2 or 3 days), dig a hole to see where the extent of wet soil is. You will be able to calculate from this how much water you need to apply to wet the soil to the bottom of the root zone. If the soil is crusted or compacted, cultivate the soil around the plant before watering. To help conserve soil moisture, apply a mulch around the plant, or incorporate peat moss or other organic matter into the soil. Do not allow the plant to wilt between waterings. Learn the water requirements of your plant so you can water properly.

Rhizoctonia stem rot

Rhizoctonia stem rot on dianthus.

Healthy chrysanthemum unaffected by rhizoctonia.

Problem: The leaves turn pale and wilt, sometimes suddenly. The lower leaves are rotted. The stem is slimy and decayed. Minute black pellets may be just barely visible around the base of the plant.

Plants: Many flowering plants, especially dianthus, vinca, moss rose, impatiens, chrysanthemum, snapdragon, sweet alyssum, and salvia.

Analysis: Stem rot is a plant disease caused by a fungus *(Rhizoctonia solani)* found in most soils. It penetrates the plant at or just below the soil level, rotting through the outer stem bark into the inner stem tissue. Unlike the soft, outer stem rot, the inner stem tissue becomes dry and corky when infected. As the rot progresses up the stem, the lower leaves rot, the foliage pales and withers, and the plant may die. Rhizoctonia thrives in warm, moist conditions.

Solution: If all the foliage is wilted, it is best to replace the plant. Plants not so severely affected can sometimes be saved, but will often worsen and die. An effective cultural method to help control the disease is to let the soil dry out between waterings. Before planting the following year, spray or dust the soil with a fungicide containing PCNB. If plants are in containers, you can try this drying-out technique. Stop watering infected plants. To dry the soil as quickly as possible, place the containers in a well-ventilated, even breezy location in full sun. But if the roots are damaged badly enough that plants wilt or drop leaves, don't put them in the sun. Eventually the soil will dry out to the point where the plants would normally need another watering. Allow the soil to become drier still to stop the fungi from continuing their decay. Take steps to minimize the water needs of the plants, such as placing the container in shade. Begin watering again when the plant shows signs of drought stress, such as heavy wilting or yellowing and dropping of leaves.

Root and stem rots

Root and stem rot on sedum.

Root and stem rot on sweet alyssum.

Problem: The plant may suddenly wilt and die, or it may die slowly from the top down. The leaves turn yellow, wilt, and eventually die, and overall growth is stunted. There may be lesions on the stems or white fungal strands on infected stems around the base of the plant. These strands may eventually develop small black or brown pellets. The roots are decayed and may turn reddish on some plants. The roots and lower part of the stems may be soft and rotten. The crown may be water-soaked and blackish brown.

Plants: Many flowering plants, especially snapdragon, bachelor's button, gerbera, sweet alyssum, sedum, and viola.

Analysis: Root and stem rot is a disease caused by several different fungi that live in the soil. These fungi thrive in waterlogged, heavy soils and are sometimes called water molds. They can attack the plant stems and roots directly or enter them through wounds. Infection causes stems and roots to decay, resulting in wilting, yellowing leaves, and plant death. Gardeners frequently mistake this wilting for drought stress and water more heavily, speeding the demise of the plants. These fungi are generally spread by infested soil and transplants, contaminated equipment, and moving water. Many of these organisms also cause damping-off of seedlings *(see page 86)*. Root rot is most severe in heavy, poorly drained soil and generally moist conditions.

Solution: Remove and discard severely infected plants. Let the soil dry out between watering. Avoid future root rot problems by planting in well-drained soil or choosing plants that can tolerate heavy soil better. Improve soil drainage by working organic matter into heavy soils.

Root problems

Snapdragons wilting from root damage.

Root-damaged pincushion flowers.

Problem: The plant is wilting. The leaves are discolored to yellow or brown and may be dying. The soil may be moist or dry.

Plants: All annuals, perennials, and biennials.

Analysis: These symptoms are caused by one of several root problems.

1. Stem and root rot: Many fungi and bacteria decay plant roots and stems. In addition to leaf wilting and discoloration, spots and lesions frequently form on the leaves and stems. The infected tissue may be soft and rotted, and the plant pulls out of the ground easily. Most of the disease-causing organisms thrive in wet soil.

2. Fertilizer burn: Excessive fertilizer causes leaves to wilt and become dull and brown. Later they become dark brown or black and dry. When too much fertilizer is applied, a concentrated solution of fertilizer salts is formed in the soil. This solution makes it difficult for plants to absorb the water they need and may even draw water out of the plant. A high concentration can cause roots to die and can lead to the death of the entire plant.

3. Nematodes: These microscopic worms live in the soil and feed on plant roots. They inject a toxin into the roots so that roots can't supply adequate water and nutrients to the aboveground plant parts. The plant slowly dies. Infested plants are weak and slow growing, often turn bronze or yellowish, and wilt on hot, dry days. If you pull the plant up, you see stunted roots that are often dark and stubby and may have nodules on them.

Solution: Solutions below correspond to the numbered items in the analysis above.

1. Look up your plant in the index to determine which stem and root rot diseases may affect it. Treat accordingly.

2. Dilute the fertilizer in the soil by watering the soil heavily. Soak the affected area thoroughly with plain water, let it drain, then soak again. Repeat 3 or 4 times. Cut off dead plant parts. Follow directions carefully when fertilizing.

3. If you have a chronic problem with wilting, yellowing plants that slowly die and if you've eliminated other possibilities, test for nematodes. Testing roots and soil is the only positive method for confirming the presence of these pests. Contact your local county extension office for sampling instructions, addresses of testing laboratories, and control procedures for your area.

Verticillium wilt

Verticillium wilt on chrysanthemum.

Verticillium wilt on sunflower.

Problem: Leaves yellow, wilt, and die, starting with the lower leaves and progressing up the plant. Older plants may be stunted. Leaf wilting and death often affect only one side of the plant. Flowering is poor. Dark brown areas may be on the infected stems. When the stem is sliced open near the base of the plant, dark streaks and discoloration of the water-conducting stem tissue are revealed. Sunflowers often show no symptoms until they flower.

Plants: Many flowering plants, especially chrysanthemum, sunflower, gloriosa daisy, and salvia.

Analysis: Verticillium wilt disease affects many ornamental plants. It is caused by a soil-inhabiting fungus *(Verticillium* species) that persists indefinitely on plant debris or in the soil. The disease spreads through contaminated seeds, plants, soil, equipment, and groundwater. The fungus enters the plant through the roots and spreads up into the stems and leaves through the water-conducting vessels in the stems. These vessels become discolored and plugged. This plugging cuts off the flow of water to the leaves, causing leaf yellowing and wilting.

Solution: No chemical control is available. It is best to destroy infected plants. Verticillium can be removed from the soil only by fumigation or solarization techniques. The best solution is to plant flowers that are resistant to verticillium.

Wilt and stem rot

Wilt and stem rot on marigold.

Healthy marigold transplants with strong roots.

Problem: Leaves wilt and die. The lower stems have a dark, water-soaked appearance. They eventually shrivel and turn brown near the soil line. The plant pulls up easily to reveal rotted roots. The plant usually dies within 1–3 weeks.

Plants: Many flowering plants are affected, especially marigold.

Analysis: Wilt and stem rot is a disease caused by a widespread fungus *(Phytophthora cryptogea)* that persists indefinitely in the soil. The fungus attacks the roots, then spreads up into the stems. As the roots and stems decay, the leaves wilt and turn yellow, and the plant dies. The fungus thrives in cool, waterlogged soils. This disease is spread by contaminated soil, moving water, transplants, and equipment. African marigolds *(Tagetes erecta)* are susceptible, but French marigolds *(T. patula)* and other dwarf varieties are resistant to this fungus.

Solution: Discard infected plants and the soil immediately surrounding them. Let the soil dry out between waterings. Plant marigolds in well-drained soil. Drench infected flowerbeds with a fungicide containing captan to help reduce the severity or chances of return of the disease. Plant resistant French and dwarf marigolds. If plants are in containers, you can try this drying-out technique. Stop watering infected plants. To dry the soil as quickly as possible, place the containers in a well-ventilated, even breezy location in full sun. But if the roots are damaged badly enough that plants wilt or drop leaves, don't put them in the sun. Eventually the soil will dry out to the point where the plants would normally need another watering. Allow the soil to become drier still to stop the fungi from continuing their decay. Take steps to minimize the water needs of the plants, such as placing the container in shade. Begin watering again when the plant shows signs of drought stress, such as heavy wilting or yellowing and dropping of leaves.

Wilt disease

Wilt disease on dahlia seedlings.

Wilt-infected salvia plant, on left.

Problem: The lower leaves turn yellow, wilt, and die; or all of the foliage may turn yellow and then wither. Older plants may be stunted. Yellowing and wilting often affect only one side of the plant. Flower heads droop. There may be dark brown areas on the infected stem. When the stem is split open near the base of the plant, dark streaks and discoloration are seen on the inner water-conducting stem tissue. The root system may be partially or entirely decayed.

Plants: Many flowering plants, especially dahlia and African daisy *(Dimorphotheca)*.

Analysis: Wilt disease affects many ornamental plants. It is caused by either of two soil-inhabiting fungi *(Verticillium dahliae* or *Fusarium* spp.) that persist indefinitely on plant debris or in the soil. Fusarium thrives in warm soils, and is more severe in the southern states. Verticillium is more of a problem in the cooler soils of the northern states. Both fungi infect all types of flowers. The disease spreads through contaminated seeds, plants, soil, and equipment. The fungus enters the plant through the roots and spreads into the stems through the water-conducting vessels in the stems. The vessels become discolored and plugged. This plugging cuts off the flow of water to the leaves, causing leaf yellowing and wilting.

Solution: No chemical control is available. It is best to destroy infected plants. Verticillium and fusarium can be removed from the soil only by fumigation or solarization techniques. The best solution is to use plants that are resistant to verticillium and fusarium wilt diseases.

SLOW OR DEFORMED PLANT GROWTH
Cyclamen mites

Cyclamen mite damage on delphinium.

Cyclamen mite damage to stem tip.

Problem: Flower buds are deformed and blackened. They may not open, or the flowers may be distorted and shriveled. The leaves are curled, cuplike, wrinkled, thickened, and brittle and may have a purplish discoloration. The plant may be stunted to only a quarter of its normal size.

Plants: Many flowering plants are affected, especially delphinium.

Analysis: Cyclamen mites (*Steneotarso-nemus pallidus*) are microscopic pests. These members of the spider family are ¹⁄₁₀₀ of an inch long and can be seen only with a hand lens. Although the mites are not visible to the unaided eye, their damage is distinctive. Mites generally live and feed in leaf and flower buds and rarely venture onto exposed plant surfaces. These pests crawl from one overlapping leaf to another. They are also spread on contaminated tools, clothing, and hands of gardeners. Cyclamen mites are seldom active during the hot summer months. They are most injurious from early spring until June and again in late summer, with the greatest damage occurring in periods of high humidity.

Solution: Spray infested plants with Ortho® Systemic Insect Killer or Ortho® Rose & Flower Insect Killer; respray 2 more times at intervals of 7–10 days. Spray the foliage thoroughly, covering both the upper and lower surfaces of the leaves. Space plants far enough apart so that their foliage doesn't overlap. This discourages the mites from spreading. Wash your hands and tools after working on an infested plant to prevent spreading mites to healthy plants.

Insufficient light or leggy growth

Weak, leggy growth on rosebud impatiens.

Elongated stems of geranium growing in low light.

Problem: The plant grows slowly or not at all and is located in a shaded area. Growth is weak and leggy, and flowering is poor. The leaves may be dark green and larger than normal. The oldest leaves may drop off. No signs of disease or insect pests are present.

Plants: All flowering plants, especially chrysanthemum and those that require full sun for best growth.

Analysis: Plants contain chlorophyll, which uses sunlight to produce energy. This energy is used to make food for plant growth and development. Plants differ in the amount of light they need to grow properly. Some plants need many hours of direct sunlight daily, while others thrive in shaded locations. Any plant that receives less light than it requires can't produce as much food as it needs. It grows slowly and is weak and leggy. Some chrysanthemum varieties grow tall and leggy naturally.

Solution: Learn the light requirements for your plant. If your plant is not receiving enough sunlight, transplant it to a sunnier location and choose a plant that requires less light for this location. Chrysanthemum plants that are leggy may be pinched back to encourage bushier growth as long as they have not yet formed flower buds. The following year, when new plants are 6–8 inches tall, carefully pinch or nip off the young growing tips just above a leaf. The tiny side bud located between this leaf and the stem will grow into a new branch. Every two weeks, pinch back all the new growing points that have formed as a result of the previous pinching. Stop pinching the plant by August to let flower buds develop. Consider replanting with mum varieties that grow low naturally.

Mealybugs

Mealybugs feeding on plant stem.

Ants attracted to honeydew from mealybugs.

Problem: White, oval insects up to ¼ inch long form white, cottony masses on the stems and leaves. Leaves may be deformed and withered. The infested leaves are often shiny and sticky or covered with a sooty mold. Ants may be present.

Plants: Many flowering plants, especially begonia and coleus.

Analysis: Mealybugs damage plants by sucking sap, causing leaf distortion and death. The adult female mealybug may produce young or deposit her eggs in white, fluffy masses of wax. The immature mealybugs, called nymphs, are very active and crawl on the plant. Soon after the nymphs begin to feed, they exude filaments of white wax that cover their bodies, giving them a cottony appearance. As they mature, their mobility decreases. Mealybugs can't digest all the sugar in the sap, and they excrete the excess in a fluid called honeydew, which coats the leaves. Ants may feed on the honeydew. Mealybugs are spread by the wind, which may blow egg masses and nymphs from plant to plant. Ants may also move them, or nymphs may crawl to nearby plants. Mealybug eggs and some adults can survive the winter in warm climates. Spring reinfestations in colder areas come from infested new plants placed in the garden.

Solution: Spray infested plants with Ortho® Rose & Flower Insect Killer or Ortho® Systemic Insect Killer (do not use on begonias). Spray at intervals of 7–10 days until the mealybugs are gone. Gently hose down plants to knock off mealybugs and wash off honeydew. Remove and destroy severely infested leaves and plants.

Poor growth

Undersized zinnias planted too late.

Phosphorus-deficient foliage of chrysanthemum.

Problem: The plant fails to grow, or it grows very slowly. No signs of insects or diseases are present.

Plants: All annuals, perennials, biennials, and bulbs.

Analysis: A plant might grow slowly for many reasons.

1. Improper planting time: Many plants require warm temperatures and long hours of sunlight to grow well. If transplants that need warm weather are set out too early in the spring or too late in the fall, when temperatures are cool, they will not grow.

2. Unseasonable cool spell: If the weather is unseasonably cool or cloudy, most plants—even those adapted to cool temperatures—will slow down their growth rate.

3. Natural dormancy: Many perennials and bulbs undergo a period of no growth soon after they have flowered. Although the plant may seem to be inactive, it is developing roots, bulbs, or rhizomes for the following year's growth. The foliage of many perennials and bulbs eventually dies back completely, and the plant becomes dormant.

4. Phosphorus deficiency: Phosphorus is a plant nutrient essential to normal plant growth and development. Many garden soils are deficient in phosphorus. When plants do not receive enough phosphorus, they usually grow very slowly or stop growing altogether. Sometimes their foliage also turns dark green, or it may redden slightly.

Solution: Solutions below correspond to the numbered items in the analysis above.

1. Learn the proper planting time for your flowers. As the weather warms up, the plants will start to grow.

2. Plants will start to grow again when unseasonable cool spells have passed. Check for signs of disease. Fungal and bacterial infections are especially troublesome during periods of moist weather.

3. Learn the life cycle of your perennial plant to determine if it has a natural dormancy period.

4. For a quick response, spray the leaves with Miracle-Gro® Bloom Booster. Fertilize the plants with the same fertilizer, which is high in phosphate.

Poor growth on bulbs

Fertilizing tulips at planting time.

Allow bulb foliage to yellow and die naturally.

Problem: Spring bulbs produce little growth in the spring.

Plants: All spring bulbs, especially tulips.

Analysis: 1. Lack of cooling: Bulbs require a period of cooling to develop properly. The length of this period varies with each type of bulb. Tulips need to spend at least 15 weeks below 50°F for proper development. If new bulbs are not precooled, or if soil temperatures remain at 55°F or above during the winter, root formation, flower emergence, and the production of new daughter bulbs for future flowering are inhibited.
2. Foliage removed too soon: After a bulb flowers, the remaining foliage uses the sun's rays to manufacture food for the developing bulbs and the following year's flowers. If the foliage is removed before it turns yellow naturally, the new bulbs are very small.
3. Lack of nutrients: After the first year, tulips don't perform well when planted in infertile soil. They form only weak, small bulbs and flowers. After several years, they stop producing growth.
4. Root rot: Infected bulbs planted in heavy, poorly drained soils frequently decay.
5. Rodents: Mice, pocket gophers, and other rodents may feed on bulbs. Dig where the bulbs were planted to check for underground tunnels and half-eaten bulbs. Both indicate rodent damage.

Solution: 1. In warm-winter areas (Zones 9 and 10; *see page 5* for zone map), refrigerate newly purchased bulbs to satisfy their cold requirement.
2. Allow foliage to turn yellow before removing it.
3. Fertilize emerging tulips with Scotts® Bulb Slow Release Plant Food in the spring and once a month after the plants have flowered until the foliage dies back.
4. Before planting, discard discolored, spongy, or moldy bulbs. Plant healthy bulbs in well-drained soil at the proper planting time.
5. The most effective method of protecting bulbs is to plant them in baskets made of ½-inch wire mesh or to line the entire planting bed with mesh before planting. To prevent mouse damage, lay ½-inch hardware cloth on top of the bulb planting area, burying the edges several inches under the soil surface. Remove the hardware cloth before shoots emerge in the spring. Traps and baits may also be used.

Root nematodes

Root nematode damage on astilbe.

Root nematode damage symptoms on foliage.

Problem: The plant is stunted and growing poorly. Leaves may be curled and yellowed. The plant pulls out of the ground easily.

Roots are sparse, short, and dark. Small knots ($\frac{1}{16}$ inch) may be visible on roots.

Plants: Many flowering plants, especially astilbe and hosta.

Analysis: Root nematodes are microscopic worms that live in the soil. They feed on plant roots, damaging and stunting them or causing them to become enlarged. The damaged roots can't supply sufficient water and nutrients to the aboveground plant parts, and the plant becomes stunted or slowly dies. Nematodes are found throughout the United States, especially in areas with moist, sandy loam soil. They can move only a few inches per year on their own, but they may be carried long distances by soil, water, tools, or infested plants. Laboratory testing of roots and soil is the only positive method for confirming the presence of nematodes. Contact your local county extension office for sampling instructions and addresses of testing laboratories. Problems such as poor soil structure, drought stress, overwatering, nutrient deficiency, and root rots can produce symptoms of decline similar to those caused by nematodes. Root weevils, such as the black vine weevil, may also cause similar symptoms. Eliminate these problems as causes before sending soil and root samples for testing.

Solution: No chemicals available to homeowners kill nematodes in planted soil. Nematodes can be controlled before planting, however, by soil fumigation or solarization techniques.

Short stems on spring bulbs

Short stems on hyacinths from inadequate chilling.

Short stems on tulip from lack of chilling.

Problem: Flower stalks are very short, and flowers may be smaller than normal. Sometimes only the tip of the flower stalk emerges and blooms at ground level. No signs of insects or disease are present, and the foliage appears healthy.

Plants: Hyacinth and tulip.

Analysis: Short stems are the result of warm spring temperatures, inadequate winter chilling, or a combination of both. Bulbs contain embryonic flowers and stems. A minimum number of weeks (hyacinths 6 weeks, tulips 15 weeks) of exposure to cool temperatures (45–50°F) during the winter stimulates the stem cells to elongate, causing the bud to emerge from the ground. During cool spring weather (40–50°F), the stems continue to elongate to their full length, at which point the flowers mature and open. In warm-weather areas, stems often fail to elongate properly because of inadequate chilling. During unseasonable hot spells in the spring (when air temperature reaches 60°F or higher), flowers are stimulated by heat to mature and open before the stems have entirely emerged from the ground.

Solution: You can't do anything to increase the length of the stem once the flower has matured. If warm spring temperatures are common in your area, plant bulbs in locations where they will receive direct sun in the morning or late afternoon or only filtered light. The lower air and soil temperatures in such areas should help to increase stem length. Plant single-flowered, long-stemmed tulips such as Darwin hybrids, single late-, and lily-flowered tulips. If you live in a warm-winter area, place tulip bulbs in paper bags in the fall and store them in the refrigerator for 15 weeks before planting, or buy precooled bulbs. In zones 9 and 10 (see page 5 for zone map), delay planting tulips until mid-December.

Spindly growth and poor flowering

Spindly growth and poor flowering on viola.

Spent flowers left on plant lead to poor blooming.

Problem: Leaves are small and thin, and stems are long and spindly. Flowering is poor, and flowers are small.

Plants: All flowering plants, especially pansy and viola.

Analysis: Several cultural problems may contribute to spindly growth.
1. Failure to remove old flowers: If fading flowers remain on the plant, only a few small new flowers are produced. When the old flowers are allowed to remain, the plant uses its energy to develop seeds instead of producing new flowers.
2. Inadequate light: Pansies and violas grow lanky and flower poorly when planted in deep shade. They require at least strong filtered light to grow compactly, and they flower most profusely in full sun during mild weather.
3. Old age: Pansies and violas are perennials, but in cold-winter climates, freezing temperatures kill them. In warm-winter areas, they often produce lanky, unattractive growth after the first growing season.

Solution: The numbered solutions below correspond to the numbered items in the analysis above.
1. Remove faded flowers.
2. Grow plants in full sun, part-day sun, or strong filtered light.
3. Treat pansies and violas as annuals. Plant them in the spring or fall in zones 9 and 10 (*see page 5* for zone map), and replace them when they start to decline. Pinch back the spindly stems to one-third of their height to rejuvenate rangy plants.

Spittlebugs

Spittlebug froth on columbine.

Spittlebugs on rosemary.

Problem: Masses of white, frothy foam are clustered between the leaves and stems. If the froth is removed, small, green, soft-bodied insects can be seen feeding on the plant tissue. The plant may be stunted.

Plants: Many annuals, perennials, biennials, and bulbs.

Analysis: Spittlebugs, insects also known as froghoppers, appear in the spring. Spittlebug eggs, laid in the fall, survive the winter to hatch when the weather warms in the spring. The young spittlebugs, called nymphs, produce a foamy froth that protects them from sun and predators. This froth envelops the nymphs completely while they suck sap from the tender stems and leaves. Adult spittlebugs are not as damaging as the nymphs. The adults are ¼ inch long, pale yellow to dark brown, and winged. They hop or fly away quickly when disturbed. Spittlebugs seldom harm plants, but if infestation is very heavy, plant growth may be stunted. The presence of spittlebugs on plants is usually objectionable only for cosmetic reasons.

Solution: Wash spittlebugs from plants with a garden hose. If plants are heavily infested, spray Ortho® Bug-B-Gon® Garden & Landscape Insect Killer or Ortho® Systemic Insect Killer according to label directions. Make sure that the plant is listed on the product label. Repeated treatments are rarely necessary.

DISCOLORED OR SPOTTED LEAVES: BACTERIAL
Bacterial leaf spot and blight

Bacterial leaf spot on begonia.

Bacterial leaf blight on geranium.

Problem: Small, blisterlike spots appear on leaves, stems, and flowers. They are usually tiny and angular in shape, dark in color, and may have yellow margins. Spots enlarge and run together, giving the leaf a blotchy appearance. A slimy substance may ooze from infected areas. Bacterial spots can be found on all parts of the plant and are most often promoted by warm, moist conditions.

Plants: Many annuals, perennials, biennials, and bulbs, especially begonia and geranium (*Pelargonium*).

Analysis: Several bacteria cause bacterial leaf spots and blight. The bacteria are spread by splashing water, contaminated equipment, and infected transplants. Bacteria can live in plant debris and in the soil for 3 months or more. Localized leaf infection causes early leaf drop. If the plant's water-conducting tissue is infected, the whole plant softens and collapses.

Solution: If practical, pick off and destroy spotted leaves and plant parts. If the plant is severely infected, discard it. Clean up plant debris. Avoid overhead watering. Wash your hands thoroughly after handling infected plants. Purchase only healthy plants. Don't take cuttings from plants that have shown symptoms. Disinfect tools after working with diseased plants. Space plants far enough apart to allow good air circulation. Spray valuable plants with a copper-based fungicide to prevent the spread of the disease and protect new growth.

Bacterial soft rot

Diseased hyacinth bulb, on left.

Bacterial soft rot on iris.

Problem: Iris leaves turn yellow, wilt, and die. Dieback often starts at the leaf tips and progresses downward. The entire leaf cluster may be found lying on the ground. If pulled gently, the leaf cluster sometimes lifts off the rhizome. Leaf bases and rhizomes are often rotted and foul smelling. Hyacinth bulbs that have been planted may not produce any foliage, or, if foliage is produced, the flower stalk develops but the flowers open irregularly and rot off. The entire stalk may rot at the base and fall over. If pulled gently, the leaves and flower stalk may lift off the bulb, which is soft, rotted, and filled with a white, thick, foul-smelling ooze.

Plants: Several bulbs and rhizomes, especially iris and hyacinth.

Analysis: Bacterial soft rot lives in the soil and in plant debris and thrives on moist conditions. The bacteria are spread by contaminated plant parts, soil, insects, and tools. It is a serious and common disease of bearded and other rhizomatous iris. The bacteria enter the plant through wounds in the leaves and rhizomes, which are frequently made by iris borers. As infection develops, the plant tissue decays into a soft, foul-smelling mass. Infection and rapid decay are accelerated by moist, dark conditions. Bacterial soft rot infects hyacinth bulbs both in storage and when planted in the ground. The bacteria initially penetrate and decay the upper portion of the bulb. The disease then progresses upward into the leaves and flower stalks and down through the bulb and roots. The thick ooze that accompanies the decay is filled with millions of bacteria. Bulbs that are infected before they are planted produce little, if any, growth. Even well-established, healthy plants may decay quite rapidly after they are infected, sometimes within 3–5 days. If bulbs freeze while they are in storage, they are especially susceptible to infection.

Solution: No cure exists for this disease. Remove and destroy all bulbs, plants and plant parts showing signs of decay. If only a small portion of an iris rhizome is infected, you may possibly save it by cutting off the diseased portion. Avoid wounding rhizomes and bulbs when planting or digging them up. After dividing rhizomes, let the wounds heal for a few days before replanting. Clean up iris plant debris in fall. Control iris borers. Store bulbs in a dry, cool (40–45°F) location. Plant only healthy bulbs and rhizomes in a sunny, well-drained soil and do not overwater.

DISCOLORED OR SPOTTED LEAVES: CULTURAL
Air pollution

Nasturtium foliage damaged by ozone.

Petunia flower damaged by air pollution.

Problem: The upper surfaces of leaves may be bleached, with white flecks or reddish-brown spots. Sometimes the leaves are distorted. Older leaves are affected more than new ones.

Plants: Many annuals, perennials, biennials, and bulbs.

Analysis: Some gases released into the atmosphere from cars and factories damage plants. The most common type of pollution is smog. Air pollution damage is most commonly a problem in urban areas, but it also occurs in rural areas where gardens are located downwind from factories. Some plants are severely affected and may even die. Flower production is reduced on pollution-damaged plants. The three most common pollutants are ozone, PAN *(peroxyacetyl nitrate)*, and sulfur dioxide. Ozone forms when gases produced by combustion engines and other industrial processes interact in the presence of sunlight with materials given off by automobiles, solvents, and vegetation. Ozone is common throughout the United States and is the primary air pollutant on the East Coast. Sulfur dioxide is an industrial pollutant resulting from burning sulfur-containing fuels such as coal and refining oil and from smelting ores. Many different environmental factors affect a plant's susceptibility to air pollution, including temperature, air movement, light intensity, and soil and air moisture.

Solution: Air pollution injury is usually a localized problem. Check with your neighbors to see if the same plants in their gardens have been affected similarly. Because injury from air pollutants is similar in appearance to injury from nutrient deficiencies, insects, diseases, and mites, these problems should be eliminated as causes before the damage is attributed to air pollution. Nothing can be done about effects of air pollutants. Help injured plants to recover by watering and fertilizing them regularly. In smoggy or industrial areas, research and grow plants that are tolerant of air pollution.

OR ENVIRONMENTAL
Edema

Edema on ivy geranium.

Healthy ivy geranium.

Problem: Water-soaked spots appear on the leaves. Eventually, these spots turn brown and corky. Affected leaves may turn yellow and drop off. Corky ridges may form on the stems and leafstalks. In most cases, the soil is moist and the air is cool and humid.

Plants: Many annuals, perennials, biennials, and bulbs, especially geranium *(Pelargonium)* and other annuals that require a well-drained soil.

Analysis: Edema is not caused by a pest, but rather is the result of an accumulation of water in the plant. Edema often develops when the soil is moist or wet and the atmosphere is humid and cool. Under these conditions, water is absorbed rapidly from the soil and lost slowly from the leaves, resulting in an excess amount of water in the plant. This excess water causes cells to burst. The ruptured cells eventually form spots and ridges. Edema occurs most frequently in plants grown in greenhouses and in late winter and early spring during cloudy weather.

Solution: Edema is not a serious condition in itself, but often indicates an overwatering problem. Plant geraniums and other flowers in soil that drains well, and avoid overwatering them. Use a light soilless mix in container plantings to improve drainage.

Iron deficiency

Iron-deficient chrysanthemum foliage.

Interveinal yellowing on geranium leaf.

Problem: Leaves turn pale green or yellow. The newest leaves (those at the tips of the stems) are most severely affected. Except in extreme cases, the veins of affected leaves remain green. In extreme cases, the newest leaves are small and completely white or yellow. Older leaves may remain green.

Plants: All flowering plants, especially those that require slightly acidic or acidic soil.

Analysis: Plants frequently suffer from deficiencies of iron and other minor nutrients such as manganese and zinc, elements essential to normal plant growth and development. Deficiencies can occur when one or more of these elements is depleted in the soil. Often these minor nutrients are present in the soil, but alkaline soils with a pH of 7.5 or higher or wet soil conditions cause them to form compounds that can't be used by the plant. An alkaline condition can result from excess lime application or from lime leached from cement or brick.

Solution: Spray the foliage with chelated iron fertilizer, and apply the fertilizer to the soil around the plants to correct the deficiency of minor nutrients. Correct the pH of the soil before planting by using ferrous sulfate or soil sulfur. Add 2 pounds per 100 square feet, wait 2 weeks, and then test the soil pH. Reapply these acidifying amendments until the desired pH has been attained. Maintain acidity by fertilizing with Miracid® ProSelect™ Water Soluble Plant Food. Alternately, select plants that are tolerant of alkaline soil. Maintain an acid-to-neutral pH by fertilizing with Miracid® Plant Food.

Leaf scorch

Leaf scorch on lily from low pH.

Leaf scorch on iris.

Problem: Leaves are brown around leaf margins and between veins or have dead patches in the middle. On lilies, usually the lower leaves are affected first, and when the soil is tested, it is found to be acidic.

Plants: All annuals, perennials, and bulbs, especially lilies.

Analysis: Leaf burn and leaf scorch occur when leaf cells overheat. Leaf scorch usually refers to browning and tissue death around leaf margins and between veins while leaf burn usually refers to dead patches in the middle of the leaf. When leaves dry out, the amount of water that evaporates is reduced and the leaves overheat, then burn or scorch. Sometimes entire leaves or shoots are damaged. Several conditions may cause leaf burn or leaf scorch. Leaf scorch may develop on lilies when they are growing in acid soil with a pH lower than 6.5.
Lack of water: Leaf burn and leaf scorch often occur when plant roots can't get enough water. Plants growing in dry, salty, frozen soils or areas with limited rooting may not get as much water as they need.

Too much water: Overwatered, poorly drained soils can cause burn or scorch. Roots require oxygen to function properly. Wet soils low in oxygen cause root death. As the roots die, they absorb less water.
Wind and heat: Hot, windy conditions cause burn and scorch in some plants, even when the soil is moist. Wind and heat cause water to evaporate from the leaves more quickly than it can be replaced.
Freeze damage: Leaf burn or leaf scorch may result when foliage freezes. Frozen leaf cells rupture or dry out and die.
Other factors: Diseased or damaged roots often can't supply as much water as the plant needs, resulting in leaf burn or leaf scorch. Burn and scorch can also be caused by an accumulation of salt in the leaf tissue.

Solution: Leaves damaged by leaf scorch or leaf burn won't recover. Keep plants properly watered to help reduce further damage. If possible, shade plants during very hot weather, and hose down foliage a couple of times a day. Protect shade-loving plants by providing adequate shade. Make sure the soil is moist when it freezes, and reduce chances of dehydration resulting from frozen soils by applying mulch around the base of the plant. If lilies are growing in soil with a pH below 6.5, add ground dolomitic limestone to decrease its acidity and fertilize with Scotts® Bulb Slow Release Plant Food.

Leaves discolored

Sunburn on hosta leaves.

Browning foliage of dried-out crocus plants.

Problem: Leaves turn pale green to yellow. The plant may be stunted. In many cases, leaf edges turn brown and crisp, and some leaves shrivel and die. No signs of disease or pests are present. Leaves do not discolor from the base of the plant upward as they do with nitrogen deficiency. (For information on nitrogen deficiency, *see page 49*.)

Plants: All annuals, perennials, biennials, and bulbs may be affected.

Analysis: Leaves discolor for several reasons.
1. Frequent drought stress: Plants require at least a minimal supply of water to remain healthy and grow properly. When they are allowed to dry out once or twice, they usually survive. Plants that suffer from frequent drought stress, however, undergo changes in their metabolism that result in leaf discoloration, stunting, and lack of growth. If the soil is allowed to dry out completely, the plant will die.
2. Salt buildup in the soil: Leaf browning and discoloration occur when excess salts dissolved in the soil water are taken into the plant and accumulate in the leaf tissue. Soil salts build up to damaging levels in soils that are not occasionally flushed. Salt buildup commonly occurs in arid regions of the country.
3. Sunburn: Shade-loving plants placed in a sunny location will develop discolored leaves. Sunburned leaves often develop a whitish or yellow bleached appearance. Leaves not directly exposed to the sun usually remain green and uninjured.

Solution: The numbered solutions below correspond to the numbered items in the analysis above.
1. Avoid allowing plants to wilt between waterings. Consult a reliable reference to determine the moisture needs of your plant. Provide plants with adequate water.
2. Flush out soil salts periodically by watering deeply and thoroughly.
3. Check to see whether your plant is adapted to sun or shade by consulting a reliable reference. Transplant shade-loving plants to a shady location.

Nutrient deficiency

Yellowed foliage of nitrogen-deficient impatiens.

Phosphorous-deficient chrysanthemum foliage.

Problem: Leaves are off color and plants grow poorly.
Lack of nitrogen: Leaves turn pale green, then yellow, beginning with the older leaves. Growth is slowed. Older leaves may drop. New leaves are small.
Lack of phosphorus: Plants are stunted and darker than usual. Leaves are dull and gray-green and may be tinged with magenta. Flowering is poor.
Lack of potassium: Plants grow slowly. Older leaves are mottled with yellow or pale green smudges. Edges of leaves scorch and die.

Plants: All flowering plants.

Analysis: All plants require adequate amounts of nitrogen, phosphorus, and potassium. If they are lacking, plants will show signs of deficiency. The best way to determine if your soil is lacking in nutrients is to have it tested.

Solution: Nitrogen: Fertilize with Miracle-Gro® All Purpose Plant Food. Repeat applications according to directions. Fertilize more frequently in sandy soils or where rainfall is heavy. Check that plants aren't suffering from saturated soil and even possibly root rot, as these conditions may cause plants to exhibit symptoms of nitrogen deficiency.
Phosphorous: For a quick response, spray the leaves with Miracle-Gro® Bloom Booster, which contains 52 percent phosphorous. Water the soil with the same fertilizer. Add Scotts® Natural Bone Meal with Iron to the soil, placing it within the root zone either by cultivating or tilling it in. In the future use a fertilizer that contains at least 5 percent phosphorus.
Potassium: Fertilize with Miracle-Gro® All Purpose Plant Food. After the first treatment, use a fertilizer that contains at least 5 percent potassium.

Overwatering

Overwatering damage on primrose.

Wilting caused by root damage from excess water.

Problem: Leaves turn light green or yellow. Leaf edges may turn brown, and some of the leaves may die. In many cases the plant is stunted. Flowering is poor. If the plant is pulled out of the ground, the roots are found to be soft and rotted. The soil is frequently or constantly wet.

Plants: All flowering plants, especially those requiring well-drained soil.

Analysis: Overwatering is a serious and common problem that often results in the decay and death of plant roots. Roots require oxygen to function normally. Oxygen is contained in tiny air spaces (pores) in the soil. When water is applied to the soil, the air is pushed out of the soil pores and replaced with water. If this water can't drain properly or is constantly reapplied, the soil pores remain filled with water. The roots can't absorb the oxygen they need in such saturated conditions, and they begin to decay. As the roots continue to rot, they are less able to supply the plant with nutrients and water, resulting in the decline and eventual death of the plant.

Solution: Allow the soil to dry slightly between waterings. It is critical to improve the soil drainage. If you must plant in heavy, poorly drained soil, use flowers that will grow in wet soil, such as astilbe, bugbane, cardinal flower, ferns, Japanese and Siberian iris, Joe-Pye weed, marsh marigold, monkey flower, New England aster, and sweet white violet.

DISCOLORED OR SPOTTED LEAVES: FUNGAL
Alternaria leaf spot and blight

Alternaria leaf spot on dianthus.

Alternaria blight on zinnia.

Problem: Dark purple or brown irregular-shape spots appear on the leaves and sometimes the stems. They may be surrounded by yellow-green margins. Sunken, grayish-brown dead areas may develop in the center of the spots, and spots may contain several dark concentric rings.

Individual spots enlarge and merge to form blotches. Infected leaves turn yellow, blacken, and then die. Lesions develop on stems, especially at the base. Flowers may be spotted. The leaves at the tips of infected stems may become mottled, turn yellow, and wilt. The entire plant may wilt and die.

Plants: Many annuals, perennials, biennials, and bulbs, especially carnation and pinks (*Dianthus*), geranium (*Pelargonium*), and zinnia.

Analysis: Alternaria leaf spot is caused by a fungus. Infection is most severe in wet, humid conditions and is prolonged by low fertility. Spores are spread by wind and splashing water. Infection occurs when spores germinate on wet leaves, stems, or petals. The fungus survives as spores on plant debris and on contaminated seed. It can also cause damping-off of seedlings.

Solution: Pick off and destroy infected plant parts and clean up and destroy plant debris. If plants are severely infected, spray them with Ortho® Garden Disease Control or a fungicide containing azoxystrobin or basic copper sulfate. Make sure that your plant is listed on the fungicide label before spraying. These sprays are protectants, not controls. They protect the new, healthy foliage but old leaves will remain diseased. Water early in the day so that foliage can dry thoroughly. Thin out dense plantings to allow air circulation. Grow resistant plant varieties whenever possible. Fertilize with Scotts® All Purpose Flower & Vegetable Slow Release Plant Food or Miracle-Gro® Water Soluble All Purpose Plant Food.

Black spot

Black spot on hellebore.

Remove brown foliage and plant debris.

Problem: Large round or elliptical black spots develop on both sides of the leaves. Spots also form on the stems, flower stalks, and sometimes petals. Concentric rings may form within the spots. Infected stems shrivel and topple, and flower buds and leaves growing on infected stems wilt and die. Foliage yellows and dies prematurely, and overall growth is weak and sparse.

Plants: Christmas rose and Lenten rose.

Analysis: Black spot is a plant disease caused by a fungus *(Coniothyrium hellebori)* that infects only hellebores. The fungal spores are spread from plant to plant by wind and splashing water. If the foliage is wet, the spores germinate and infect leaf, stem, and petal tissue. Black spot thrives in moist conditions. In wet, humid weather, black spot can spread through an entire planting in several days. The fungus survives the winter in infected plant debris.

Solution: Remove dying plants and plant debris. Cut off and destroy all diseased plant parts. Spray with a fungicide containing captan at intervals of 10–14 days until the spotting no longer occurs. Resume spraying during wet weather.

Bud rot

Bud rot on canna.

Plant only healthy canna rhizomes.

Problem: The newly opened young leaves may be partially or entirely black, or they may be covered with tiny white spots. The older leaves may be distorted and are often covered with yellow or brown spots and streaks. In many cases, the flower buds turn black and die before they open. Entire stalks are often decayed. A sticky substance may coat infected leaf tissue.

Plants: Canna.

Analysis: Bud rot is a plant disease caused by bacteria (*Xanthomonas* species) that usually attack the young canna leaves and flowers while they are still curled in the buds. The bacteria can spread from the leaves and flowers into the stems, causing plant death. Some of the infected tissue may exude sticky ooze filled with bacteria. The bacteria are spread by splashing water and rain and by direct contact with equipment, hands, and insects. Wet conditions enhance the spread of the disease. Bud rot survives through the winter in diseased rhizomes, contaminated soil, and infected plant debris.

Solution: There are no effective chemical controls for this disease. To control bud rot, it is important to reduce excess moisture around the plants. Water in the morning so the foliage will dry out during the day. Avoid wetting the foliage. Space plants far enough apart to allow good air circulation. Pick off infected leaves and flowers. Remove severely diseased plants and the soil immediately surrounding them. Clean up plant debris. Plant only healthy plants and rhizomes. Rhizomes should be firm, without wounds or blemishes. They should not be moldy or dried. Container plants should have large, healthy leaves of good color, be free of spots or dead areas, and should not have been recently pruned.

Crown rot or wilt

Crown rot on columbine.

Crown rot on iris.

Problem: Leaves and stems are stunted, yellowing, and wilting. The diseased branches slowly dry out, starting at the leaf tips and progressing downward, and finally die. On iris, leaf bases and possibly the rhizomes are dry, brown, and rotted. White fungal strands may grow on the stems of severely infected plants. When sliced open, an infected stem or rhizome may be filled with white fungal threads and small black fungal pellets. The soil around the plant may be filled with white fungal strands and reddish-brown spherical pellets the size of a pinhead.

Plants: A wide variety of flowering plants, especially columbine, iris, and delphinium.

Analysis: Crown rot or wilt is caused by various Sclerotinia fungi that live in the soil. The fungi survive the winter as fungal strands and dormant pellets in plant debris or in the soil. It is favored by high humidity, crowded plantings, and moist soils and attacks plant roots or stem tissue at the soil line. Sclerotinia produces windblown spores in the spring and summer that may also infect the foliage. As the fungus spreads within the plant, wilting and eventually death occur. Sclerotinia can persist in the soil for 3 years or more. It is spread by infested soil transplants, moving water, and contaminated tools.

Solution: Remove and destroy diseased plants and rhizomes and discard the soil immediately around them to 6 inches beyond the diseased area. Plant only healthy rhizomes and plants. Plant in well-drained soil with roots covered and rhizomes showing through the top of the soil. Let the soil dry out between waterings. Cultivate the soil around the crown of the plant to help it dry out more quickly. Thin out overcrowded plantings.

Foxglove anthracnose

Leaf symptoms of foxglove anthracnose.

Collecting foxglove seeds to start new plants.

Problem: Light or purplish-brown spots up to ⅛ inch appear on the leaves. The spots are circular or angular and have purplish margins. Often black, rough areas develop in the centers of the leaf spots. Sunken lesions may occur on the leaf veins and stems, and severely infected leaves turn yellow, wither, and drop off. Often plants are stunted and die, especially during periods of warm, moist weather. Seedlings may wilt and die.

Plants: Foxglove (*Digitalis*).

Analysis: Foxglove anthracnose is a plant disease caused by a fungus (*Colletotrichum fuscum*) that infects only foxgloves. The fungal spores are spread from plant to plant by splashing water or rain, insects, animals, and contaminated tools. If the leaves are wet, the spores germinate and infect the leaf tissue, creating spots and lesions. Warm temperatures and moist conditions favor development of foxglove anthracnose. The fungus survives the winter in diseased plant debris and infected seed. This fungus also causes damping-off of foxglove seedlings.

Solution: If practical, pick off infected leaves. Treat with a fungicide containing azoxystrobin. Repeat at 7- to 14-day intervals as long as conditions are favorable for the disease. Water in the morning so the foliage will have a chance to dry out. Avoid wetting the foliage when watering. Remove and destroy plant debris at the end of the growing season. The following year, plant foxglove in a different bed, with plants spaced far enough apart to allow good air circulation. There are several things you can do to prevent damping-off of seedlings. Incorporate sand or perlite into the soil mix to increase drainage. Don't add fertilizers that are high in nitrogen until seedlings have produced at least one pair of true leaves. Encourage rapid growth by planting seeds in soil that is the proper temperature for rapid germination. Provide germinating seedlings with bright light and good air circulation. Coating seeds with a fungicide containing captan will help discourage damping-off. Cover seeds started indoors with a thin (⅛- to ¼-inch) layer of sphagnum peat moss.

Fungal leaf and flower spots

Fungal leaf spot on impatiens.

Alternaria fungal leaf spot on geranium.

Problem: Spots and blotches appear on the leaves and/or flowers. The spots range in size from barely visible to an inch in diameter or more. They may be yellow, red, tan, gray, brown, or black. Several spots may join to form large blotches. Often the infected leaves are yellow and dying. Spotting is sometimes accompanied by oozing, leaf yellowing, wilting, and decay. In damp conditions, a fine gray mold sometimes covers the infected leaf tissue. On iris, the spots have distinct reddish borders and may be surrounded by water-soaked margins that later turn yellow.

Plants: Many annuals, perennials, biennials, and bulbs, especially begonia, campanula, chrysanthemum, delphinium, daylily, heuchera, impatiens, iris, nasturtium, and viola.

Analysis: Thousands of leaf-spotting fungi exist, and most flowering plants are occasionally blemished by leaf spots. Fortunately, most leaf spots cause only cosmetic damage on flowering plants. However, they can become serious enough to eventually kill plants, especially if plants are infected several years in a row. Infection is usually most severe during moist, warm weather (50–85°F). The fungal spores are spread by splashing water, wind, insects, tools, and infected transplants and seed. The spores germinate—usually within a drop of water on the leaf surface—and enter the leaf. A spot forms wherever spores infect a leaf. Leaf spot fungi survive the winter in old infected leaves and plant debris. Fungal leaf spots should be differentiated from bacterial leaf spots before beginning any type of control. In general, fungal leaf spots are small and circular and bacterial leaf spots are usually tiny and angular in shape.

Leaf spot on nasturtium.

Septoria leaf spot.

Solution: Picking off diseased leaves may give adequate control if your plant is only lightly spotted. Remove and destroy plants that are severely infected. Clean up plant debris in fall to get rid of overwintering sites. Water early in the day so that foliage can dry thoroughly and the fungi don't have a chance to germinate on wet plant parts. Grow resistant plant varieties whenever possible. If plants are severely infected, spray them with a fungicide containing chlorothanil, such as Ortho® Garden Disease Control, or a fungicide containing mancozeb, basic copper sulfate, azoxystrobin, or iprodione. Make sure that your plant is listed on the label before spraying, and make sure your plant is infected with a fungal leaf spot rather than a bacterial leaf spot *(see page 42)*. Most fungicides are not effective on bacterial leaf spots. Time your spraying carefully. Fungicides are protectants, not controls. They protect the new, healthy foliage by providing a protective barrier on the leaf surface and preventing the spores from germinating or killing the spores before they enter the leaf. To be effective, this protective barrier must be in place before the spore lands on the leaf. The fungicide must also be renewed periodically as it wears off or as new, unprotected growth appears. Old leaves that are already infected will not be affected by the fungicide and will remain diseased. Iris leaves should be sprayed in spring as soon as new growth appears. Repeat 4–6 more times at intervals of 7–10 days. Use a spreader-sticker to make sure the fungicide adheres to the smooth iris leaves.

Fusarium yellows

Fusarium yellows on gladiolus.

Healthy gladious flower stalk.

Problem: Foliage and flower spikes are stunted, and flowers may be small and faded. Yellowing starts on the leaf tips and spreads through the entire plant, which finally dies. When the dying plant is pulled out of the ground, the roots are rotted and the corm (the "bulb" of the gladiolus plant) is spotted with circular, firm, brown, or black lesions. In some cases, the corm appears normal. When it is split open, however, brown, discolored inner tissue is revealed.

Plants: Gladiolus.

Analysis: Fusarium yellows is a very common and widespread disease of gladiolus plants and corms caused by a soil-inhabiting fungus (*Fusarium oxysporum* f. *gladioli*). The fungus may penetrate and rot the corms in storage or in the ground. Wet soils and warm temperatures (70°F and higher) promote the rapid development of this disease. Corms in storage are sometimes contaminated, but the fungal decay may not have progressed far enough to be noticed. When these corms are planted the following spring, they may not produce foliage if severely infected. If they do produce feeble growth, it soon turns yellow and dies. The fungus survives in diseased corms and soil for many years. Corms that have been removed from the soil prematurely are especially susceptible to infection.

Solution: Destroy all plants and corms that show signs of infection. Dig them up only when they have fully matured. Don't replant healthy corms in soil in which diseased plants have grown. Store corms in a dry, cool (40–50°F) place. Some varieties are less susceptible than others to fusarium yellows.

Gray mold

Gray mold on begonia leaf.

Gray mold on peony flower.

Problem: Brown spots and blotches appear on leaves and possibly on stems of infected plants. As the disease progresses, a fuzzy brown or grayish mold forms on the infected tissue. Gray mold and spots often appear on the flowers, especially during periods of cool, wet weather. The leaves and stems may be soft and rotted. In some plants, gray mold leads to cankers or rots of stems, roots, corms, and bulbs. Gray mold is a common disease of peonies, causing new shoots to wilt and die and young flower buds to turn black and wither. The bases of the stems are brownish black and rotted. Older buds and open flowers turn soft and brown and develop a gray or brown fuzzy covering in wet weather. This distinctive fuzzy growth, which may develop on all infected plant parts, helps distinguish gray mold from phytophthora blight on peony (*see page 61*), with which it is sometimes confused.

Plants: Many annuals, perennials, biennials, and bulbs, especially floss flower (*Ageratum*), begonia, carnation and pinks (*Dianthus*), peony, geranium (*Pelargonium*), petunia, marigold (*Tagetes*), verbena, and zinnia.

Analysis: Gray mold, often called botrytis blight, blossom blight, or bud and flower blight, is a widespread plant disease caused by Botrytis species fungi that are found on most dead plant tissue and in most garden soils. These fungi thrive in cool, moist conditions. The fungus usually begins to grow on plant debris or weak or inactive plant tissue, such as old leaves, flowers, and overripe fruit, causing spotting and mold. The fuzzy mold that develops is composed of millions of microscopic spores. Once gray mold has become established on flowers, it can invade healthy plant tissue. The fungal spores are spread by wind or splashing water or by infected pieces of plant tissue contacting healthy tissue. Cool temperatures and high humidity promote gray mold growth. Crowded plantings, rain, and overhead watering also enhance the spread of the disease. Infection is more likely in spring and fall, when temperatures are lower. In warm-weather areas where freezing is rare, gray mold can be a year-round problem.

(continued on next page)

Gray mold (continued)

Gray mold on petunia flower.

Gray mold on marigold flower.

Solution: The key to avoiding problems with gray mold is good sanitation. Remove and destroy dying or infected leaves, stems, and flowers, especially those in contact with damp soil, so the fungus will not produce the thousands of spores necessary to infect healthy plants. Clean up and destroy plant debris in fall; do not put infected plant parts in the compost pile. Provide enough space between plants to allow good air circulation so the foliage can dry quickly after rain. Place susceptible plants in areas that receive morning sun and have good air movement (i.e., away from a fence or building). Improve air circulation by pruning branches to make the plant more open or by thinning out some plants to reduce crowding. Water plants at soil level to avoid wetting the foliage when watering. Apply a soil mulch to help prevent the soil from splashing up on the plant during rain. Spray infected plants with Ortho® Garden Disease Control or a fungicide containing mancozeb at regular intervals of 10–14 days for as long as mold is visible. Spray emerging peony shoots if the disease was severe the year before. Make sure your plant is listed on the product label.

Phytophthora blight

Phytophthora blight on vinca.

Peony plants infected with phytophthora blight.

Problem: Leaves shrivel and turn brownish green, then brown or black. Eventually the entire plant collapses. The roots are healthy. On peonies, new shoots wilt and turn black. Flowers, buds, leaves, and stems shrivel and turn dark brown and leathery. Black lesions several inches long often appear on lower sections of the stems. The plant pulls up easily. Roots are black and rotted. The fuzzy growth of gray mold *(see pages 59 and 60)* does not occur in this disease.

Plants: A wide variety of annuals, perennials, and biennials, especially vinca *(Catharanthus)*, peony, and periwinkle.

Analysis: Phytophthora blight is caused by a soil-borne fungus *(Phytophthora* spp.) that infects a wide variety of garden plants. It is the most serious disease of periwinkle, capable of killing a plant in two weeks, and it is a serious problem on peonies as well. The fungus can survive in the soil for many years. It attacks only the stems and leaves on periwinkle but it will attack roots on peonies and other plants. The spores are splashed by rain or watering drops onto the plant tops. Peonies suffer attack at the roots or at the developing shoots at the soil level, causing shoot wilting and a dark decay of the stem tissue. This fungus is promoted by waterlogged soils and humid or wet weather. During hot, wet conditions, phytophthora blight can destroy whole beds in a short time.

Solution: Infected periwinkle plants can't be cured. To avoid future problems, mulch the bed to avoid splashing spores onto the plants. Space plants far enough apart to allow good air circulation. Use drip irrigation if possible. If you use overhead watering, do it early enough in the day that the plants will dry quickly. In the future, select tolerant flowers for this spot. Peonies can be protected by spraying or drenching the soil with a fungicide containing mancozeb. Spray 3 times at intervals of 5–10 days. Reapply if infection recurs. Thin out overcrowded plants. Plant peonies in well-drained soil.

Powdery mildew

Powdery mildew on garden phlox.

Powdery mildew on verbena.

Problem: Powdery grayish-white spots and patches cover the leaves and stems, often primarily the upper surfaces of leaves.

Infected leaves eventually turn yellow and dry. The fungus can kill whole branches and entire plants.

Plants: Many annuals, perennials, biennials, and bulbs, especially aster, begonia, bee balm, black-eyed Susan, chrysanthemum, cineraria, dahlia, delphinium, hollyhock, ranunculus, sunflower, sweet pea, phlox, verbena, and zinnia.

Analysis: Powdery mildew, one of the most common plant diseases, is caused by several closely related fungi that thrive in both humid and dry weather. The powdery patches consist of fungal strands and spores. Unlike most other fungal plant diseases, powdery mildew grows on the outside of leaves, forming a white or gray "powder". The spores are spread by the wind to healthy plants. The fungus saps plant nutrients, causing the leaves to turn yellow and sometimes to die. A severe infection may kill the plant. Since some powdery mildews attach to many different kinds of plants, the fungus from a diseased plant may infect other types of plants. Under certain conditions, powdery mildew can spread through a closely spaced planting in a matter of days. In the late summer and fall, the fungus forms small, black, spore-producing bodies that are dormant during the winter but which can infect more plants the following spring. Powdery mildew is generally most severe in the late spring and early fall when the days are warm, nights are cool, and rainfall is light. The heaviest outbreaks often occur in humid, shaded sites. Unlike other fungal diseases, which only infect wet leaves, powdery mildew invades dry as well as wet leaves. This trait makes it the only fungal leaf disease that is active during dry weather.

Profusion zinnias are resistant to powdery mildew.

Powdery mildew on zinnia foliage.

Solution: Remove and destroy severely infected plants. Where practical, pick off diseased leaves. Clean up and destroy plant debris. Plant susceptible plants in sites that have good air movement and receive early morning sun. Provide good air circulation by pruning branches to make the plant more open or by thinning to avoid crowding. Pruning overhanging trees and shrubs to improve air circulation and sunlight penetration also will help slow the spread of disease. Maintaining a slow, even growth rate with light, frequent nitrogen applications will help suppress disease development. Avoid fall nitrogen fertilizer applications, which stimulate new mildew-sensitive growth. Several different fungicides can be used to prevent the spread of powdery mildew, including Ortho® Garden Disease Control and fungicides containing wettable sulfur, lime, or copper. Make sure that your plant is listed on the fungicide label before spraying. Spray fungicides at regular intervals of 10–14 days or as often as necessary to protect new growth. Fungicides protect new, healthy foliage but will not eradicate the fungus on leaves that are already infected. Spraying with an antitranspirant, or antidesiccant, may also help prevent infection. This is a spray that coats the leaf with a thin plastic film that acts as a barrier against the fungus. Plant breeders have put a high priority on developing mildew-resistant varieties, and these should be used whenever possible. Bee balms showing resistance include 'Marshall's Delight', 'Raspberry Wine', 'Gardenview Scarlet', and 'Violet Queen'. Powdery mildew-resistant phloxes include 'David', 'Chattahoochee', 'Morris Berd', and 'Spring Delight'. Zinnia cultivars resistant to powdery mildew include 'Blue Point', 'Oklahoma', and the Profusion and Pinwheel series.

Rust

Rust on geranium.

Hollyhock rust shows up first on lower leaves.

Problem: Yellow or orange spots appear on the upper surfaces of leaves. The most obvious symptoms are the orange-brown pustules of spores that develop on the undersides of leaves, which are characteristic signs of a rust infection. These pustules may also form on the upper side of the leaves, on stems, and on green flower parts. Infected leaves usually dry up and die. Rust diseases tend to become more severe as the summer progresses, killing most of the leaves on infected plants by early fall.

Plants: Many annuals, perennials, biennials, and bulbs, especially hollyhock, snapdragon, chrysanthemum, carnation and pinks *(Dianthus)*, iris, and annual geranium *(Pelargonium)*.

Analysis: The plant disease rust is caused by any of several related fungi. Most rust fungi spend the winter as spores on living plant tissue and, in some cases, in plant debris. Rust spores may be blown hundreds of miles to infect healthy plants. Some rust fungi also infect various weeds, trees, and shrubs during part of their life cycle. If you know what these alternate hosts are, you can reduce rust infection by eliminating these hosts, if possible. Flower infection usually starts in the spring as soon as conditions are favorable for plant growth. Splashing water and wind spread the spores to healthy plants. Some rust fungi can't infect the flower host unless the foliage is wet for 6–8 hours. Rust is favored by moist weather, cool nights, and warm days. Most rusts require a living host to survive the winter; others can survive on plant debris.

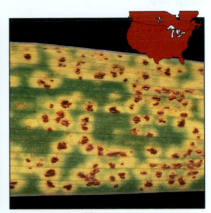

Rust pustules on chrysanthemum.

Close-up of rust on iris.

Solution: Several different fungicides are used to control rust, including Ortho® Garden Disease Control and fungicides containing triadimefon, azoxystrobin, and mancozeb. Make sure that your plant is listed on the fungicide label before spraying. Spray plants in the spring as soon as the first signs of infection are noticed. Spray the foliage thoroughly, being sure to cover both the upper and lower surfaces of the leaves. The fungicide protects the new, healthy foliage but will not eradicate the fungus on diseased leaves. Spray once every 7–10 days or as often as necessary to protect new growth until the end of the growing season. Some plants are so susceptible to rust that you may need to spray at weekly intervals throughout the summer. Fungicides will protect only uninfected tissues; they will not cure diseased leaves. To try to break the disease cycle, it is important to remove and destroy all infected foliage in the fall when the plant has stopped growing and again in early spring. Pick off and destroy infected plant parts during the growing season when plants are dry. Space plants far enough apart for good air circulation, and try to keep foliage dry. This may mean thinning out some plants. Hand water at the base of the plants, or use soaker hoses to keep leaves dry when watering. If you must use overhead watering, water in the morning rather than in the late afternoon or evening to allow wet foliage to dry out more quickly. Plant rust-resistant varieties when available. Chrysanthemums that show resistance to rust include 'Achievement', 'Copper Bowl', 'Escapade', 'Helen Castle', 'Mandalay', 'Matador', 'Miss Atlanta', 'Orange Bowl', and 'Powder Puff'. On geraniums, rust is only a significant problem on florist geraniums (*Pelargonium* ×*hortorum*), especially the zonal types. Ivy geranium (*P. peltatum*), Martha Washington or regal (*P.* ×*domesticum*), the scented-leaf types, and the wild geraniums are resistant. There are no hollyhocks available that are completely resistant to rust, but Happy Lights Mixture has shown some resistance.

Tulip fire

Infected tulip leaves and flower.

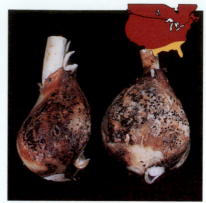

Shrunken lesions on bulb.

Problem: Light- to dark-colored spots appear on the leaves and flowers. Spots enlarge to form extensive gray blotches, which may cover the entire leaf and flower. During periods of cool, moist weather, a fuzzy brown or grayish mold forms on the infected tissue. Many of the leaves and stems are distorted, and they often rot off at the base. Dark, circular, sunken lesions appear on infected bulbs. Dark brown pinhead-size pellets form on the bulb husks.

Plants: Tulip.

Analysis: Tulip fire is a common disease of tulips caused by the fungus *Botrytis tulipae*. (It is also known as botrytis blight.) The fungus persists through the winter and hot, dry periods as tiny fungal pellets in the soil, plant debris, and bulbs. In the spring, these pellets produce spores that attack foliage and flowers, causing spotting, decay, and mold. Wounded, weak, and dead plant tissues are especially susceptible to infection. The fungus spreads through splashing water. Botrytis blight is most serious during periods of cool, moist weather. Tulip bulbs that are injured when dug up to be stored are especially vulnerable to infection.

Solution: Destroy diseased plants, leaves, flowers, and debris. Before planting tulip bulbs, check them for signs of infection, and discard diseased bulbs. Start spraying emerging plants when they are 4 inches tall with a fungicide containing mancozeb. Use a spreader-sticker when spraying. Spray plants every 5–7 days until flowers bloom. Remove tulip flowers just as they start to fade, and cut off the foliage at ground level when it turns yellow. Plant new bulbs in a different location the following year.

DISCOLORED OR SPOTTED LEAVES: INSECT
Aphids

Ladybugs are a natural control for aphids.

Damaged impatiens foliage caused by aphids.

Problem: Young leaves are curled, stunted, and yellowing. Flowers may be malformed. A sticky or shiny substance may coat the leaves. Tiny (⅛-inch) soft-bodied insects that range in color from pale green to dark brown or black are clustered on the leaves and stems. Ants may be present.

Plants: A wide variety of annuals, bulbs, perennials, and biennials, especially astilbe, chrysanthemum, gerbera, daylily (*Hemerocallis*), and lily.

Analysis: Aphids do little damage in small numbers. They are extremely prolific, however, and populations can rapidly build to damaging numbers during the growing season. Damage occurs when aphids suck the juices from the leaves and flower buds. Aphids are unable to digest all the sugar in the plant sap and excrete the excess in a fluid called honeydew. The honeydew often drops onto the leaves below. Ants feed on this sticky substance and are often present where there is an aphid infestation. Aphids can also be responsible for spreading viral diseases.

Solution: Spray with Ortho® Systemic Insect Killer, Ortho® Rose & Flower Insect Killer, or Ortho® Malathion Plus® Insect Spray Concentrate as soon as the insects appear. Repeat the spray if the plant is reinfested. In the fall, clean up plant debris that might harbor aphid eggs over winter.

Aster leafhoppers

Aster leafhopper damage on coreopsis.

Close-up of leafhoppers.

Problem: Pale green, winged insects, up to ⅛ inch long, usually feed on the undersides of leaves. They hop away quickly when the plant is touched. Leaves may be stippled.

Plants: A wide variety of flowers, especially aster and tickseed *(Coreopsis)*.

Analysis: The aster leafhopper *(Macrosteles fascifrons)*, also known as the six-spotted leafhopper, is an insect that feeds on many ornamental and vegetable plants. It generally feeds on the undersides of leaves, sucking the plant sap, which causes the stippling. This leafhopper can infect plants with the disease aster yellows *(see page 69)*. Leafhoppers at all stages of maturity are active throughout the growing season. Adult leafhoppers can't overwinter where temperatures approach freezing. The eggs they lay in the fall survive on perennial weeds and ornamental plants, however. The eggs hatch and the emerging insects reinfest plants when the weather warms up in the spring. Even areas that have winters so cold that the eggs can't survive are not free from infestation, because leafhoppers can migrate in the spring from warmer regions.

Solution: Spray plants with Ortho® Systemic Insect Killer Ready to Use or Ortho® Bug-B-Gon® Garden & Landscape Insect Killer, being sure to cover the undersides of leaves. Repeat the spray as necessary to keep the insects under control, allowing at least 10 days to pass between applications. Avoid spraying when bees are present. Eradicate nearby weeds that may harbor leafhopper eggs and aster yellows.

Aster yellows

Foliar symptoms of aster yellows on aster.

Deformed marigold flowers due to aster yellows.

Problem: Leaf veins pale and may lose all their color. Part or all of the foliage turns yellow. Leaf edges may turn brown. The flowers are dwarfed and distorted and may turn green. The plant may grow many thin stems bearing pale, spindly leaves. The plant is generally stunted.

Plants: A wide variety of flowering plants, especially China aster *(Callistephus)*, chrysanthemum, snapdragon, blanket flower *(Gaillardia)*, marigold *(Tagetes)*, gladiolus, pinks *(Dianthus)*, and purple coneflower *(Echinacea)*.

Analysis: Aster yellows is a plant disease caused by phytoplasmas, microscopic organisms similar to bacteria. The phytoplasmas are transmitted from plant to plant, primarily by leafhoppers. (For information on leafhoppers, *see page 68.*) The symptoms of aster yellows are more severe and appear more quickly in warm weather. Although the disease may be present in the plant, aster yellows may not manifest its symptoms in temperatures of 55°F or lower. The disease infects many ornamental plants, vegetables, and weeds.

Solution: Aster yellows can't be eliminated entirely, but it can be controlled. Remove and destroy infected ornamental plants. To remove sources of infection, eradicate nearby weeds that may harbor aster yellows and leafhopper eggs. Spray leafhopper-infested plants with Ortho® Systemic Insect Killer or Ortho® Bug-B-Gon® Garden & Landscape Insect Killer. Repeat the spray whenever leafhoppers reappear in the garden.

Four-lined plant bugs

Brown leaf spots caused by four-lined plant bug.

Four-lined plant bug feeding on foliage.

Problem: Numerous small tan or bleached spots appear on leaves. Leaves may be distorted. Flowers often drop off plants.

Plants: A wide variety of flowering plants, especially false sunflower *(Heliopsis)*, chrysanthemum, and Shasta daisy.

Analysis: Four-lined plant bugs belong to a large group of insects that infest many plants in the garden. This group includes many species of plant bugs, leaf bugs, lygus bugs, predaceous bugs, and stinkbugs. These insects are true bugs, of the order Hemiptera. They have long legs and antennae and large eyes, and the adults hold their wings flat over their bodies. Immature plant bugs often have clearly visible wing pads. Both the immature and mature bugs feed on succulent plant tissue. They pierce the tissue and remove the cell contents. The mature females may also damage plants by laying eggs inside the leaves or stems. Many plant bugs have two or more generations per year, so late-season populations can be large and damaging.

Solution: It is important to control four-lined plant bugs before they build up to damaging numbers. Watch for signs of infestation during the growing season. If damage is noticed, spray plants with Ortho® Malathion Plus® Insect Spray. Make sure that your plant is listed on the product label. If migrating plant bugs reinfest the plant, repeat the spray as necessary.

Iris borers

Iris borer damage to foliage.

Larva of iris borer.

Problem: Dark streaks, water-soaked spots, and possibly slits develop in new leaves in the spring to early summer. Leaf edges may be chewed and ragged. By midsummer, the foliage is wilting and discolored. Leaf bases are loose and rotted. Rhizomes (elongated underground stems) are often filled with holes and may be soft and rotted. Pink caterpillars 1–2 inches long are feeding inside the rhizomes.

Plants: Iris.

Analysis: Iris borer (*Macronoctua onusta*), the larva of a night-flying moth, is the most destructive insect pest of iris. In the fall, the adult moth lays 150–200 eggs in old leaf and flower stalks. The eggs hatch in late April or early May. Emerging larvae initially feed on the leaf surface, producing ragged leaf edges and watery feeding scars. They then bore into the inner leaf tissue and gradually mine their way down into the rhizome, on which they feed throughout the summer. The damaged rhizome is very susceptible to bacterial soft rot. The larvae leave the rhizome, pupate in the soil, and emerge as adult moths in the fall.

Solution: To kill the borers in lightly infested rhizomes, poke a wire into borer holes. In late spring, squeeze the leaves in the vicinity of feeding damage to kill borers feeding inside. Destroy heavily infested plants and rhizomes. Kill the larvae before they enter the leaves with an insecticide containing malathion. Spray weekly from the time growth first starts until the beginning of June. Clean up and destroy plant debris by April to eliminate overwintering borer eggs.

Leaf nematodes

Leaf nematode damage on begonia.

Leaf nematode damage on chrysanthemum.

Problem: Fan-shaped or angular yellow-brown to gray leaf blotches develop progressively upward from the lower leaves. The blotches join together, and the leaf turns brown or black. The leaf then withers, dies, and hangs along the stem. The plant is stunted, and new leaf buds don't develop. In the spring, young, succulent, leafy growth becomes thickened, distorted, and brittle.

Plants: A wide variety of flowering plants, especially begonia and chrysanthemum.

Analysis: The cause of this damage is a microscopic worm called a leaf nematode that lives and feeds inside the leaf tissue. The nematode is restricted in its movement by larger leaf veins. This confined feeding range creates the angular shape of the blotch. When the foliage is wet, the nematode migrates in the thin film of water on the outside of the leaf to infect healthy tissue. This pest is spread from plant to plant by splashing water. It penetrates the plant tissue by entering through small breathing pores on the underside of the leaf. Leaf nematodes are most damaging in warm, wet-summer regions of the country. They can survive for 3 years or more in plant debris and in soil.

Solution: Remove and destroy severely infested plants. Pick off and destroy all infested leaves and the 2 leaves directly above them. Avoid wetting the foliage as much as possible. Check new plants carefully to be sure they aren't diseased, and avoid replanting them in infested soil.

Leafminers

Leafminer damage on columbine.

Leafminer trails in chrysanthemum leaf.

Problem: Winding white or gray trails appear in the leaves. Some of the trails contain scattered black matter. Infested leaves may be almost covered by white trails. Leaves may die.

Plants: A wide variety of flowering plants, especially columbine and chrysanthemum.

Analysis: The columbine leafminer (*Phytomyza aquilegivora*) is an insect that belongs to the family of leafmining flies. The pale brown adult fly lays its eggs on the undersides of leaves. The eggs hatch, and the larvae that emerge penetrate the leaf and live between the upper and lower surfaces of the leaf. They feed on the inner leaf tissue, creating winding trails. Dark excrement may dot or partially fill sections of the trails. The larvae may be present continually from spring through fall.

Solution: Spray with Ortho® Rose & Flower Insect Killer or Ortho® Systemic Insect Killer. Respray at the first sign of further infestation. Pick off and destroy infested leaves. Remove and destroy all plant remains in the fall.

Spider mites

Spider mites and webbing.

Two-spotted spider mite damage on fuchsia.

Problem: Leaves are stippled, yellowing, and dirty. Leaves may dry out and drop. There may be fine webbing over flower buds, between leaves, or on the lower surfaces of leaves. Plants lose vigor. Discoloration is most severe during hot, dry weather. To determine if a plant is infested with two-spotted spider mites, hold a sheet of white paper underneath an affected leaf and tap the leaf sharply. Minute specks the size of pepper grains will drop to the paper and begin to crawl. These pests are easily seen against the white background. Mites can also be seen with a 10× hand lens.

Plants: A wide variety of annuals, bulbs, perennials, and biennials, especially when growing in full sun during hot, dry periods.

Analysis: Two-spotted spider mites *(Tetranychus urticae)*, related to spiders, are major pests of many garden and greenhouse plants. They cause damage by sucking sap from the undersides of leaves. As a result of their feeding, the chlorophyll disappears, producing the stippled appearance. Spider mite webbing traps cast-off skins and debris, making the plant dirty. Mites are active throughout the growing season but favor hot, dry weather (70°F and higher).

Solution: If spider mite infestations are detected early enough, a spraying with a garden hose can be an effective control. Spray the foliage thoroughly, covering both the upper and lower surfaces of the leaves. Repeat the spraying 2 more times at 7- to 10-day intervals. Treat affected plants with Ortho® Bug-B-Gon® Garden & Landscape Insect Killer or Ortho® Systemic Insect Killer. Insecticidal soap is another effective control for spider mites.

Thrips

Thrips damage on ornamental onion.

Gladiolus thrips damage.

Problem: Silvery-white streaks and flecks appear on flowers and foliage. The leaves may become papery and distorted, turning brown and dropping prematurely. Flowers may be deformed and discolored. Damage may appear in one location, then slowly spread over the plant. In early morning, late afternoon, or on overcast days, blackish-brown, slender, winged insects $\frac{1}{16}$ inch long can be seen on foliage and flower petals. On warm, sunny days the insects hide between leaves and in flower buds. They can be detected by pulling apart a flower bud or 2 overlapping leaves. Shaking a blossom or tapping a leaf over a sheet of paper may reveal the tiny insects, which hop or fly when disturbed.

Plants: A wide variety of annuals, perennials, biennials, and bulbs, especially allium, chrysanthemum, and gladiolus.

Analysis: Both the immature and adult thrips feed on plant sap by rasping the plant tissue. The injured tissue turns white, causing the characteristic streaking and silvering of the leaves and flowers. The adult female thrips inserts her eggs into mature plant tissue; the emerging young mature within 2–4 weeks. Thrips actively feed and reproduce from spring until the first frost of fall. They can't survive freezing temperatures. In warm-winter climates, adult thrips hibernate in the soil until spring. In cold-winter climates, they overwinter by hibernating in grass clumps, plant debris, and corms in storage. Gladiolus thrips (*Taeniothrips simplex*) is one of the most common insect pests of gladiolus. Corms infested by thrips turn brown and corky and may fail to grow, or they may produce only stunted, poor-quality flowers and foliage.

Solution: Thrips can be kept under control but not eliminated entirely. Spray plants before they bloom with Ortho® Systemic Insect Killer. Repeat the spray at intervals of no less than 7 days if reinfection occurs. Pick off and destroy old infected leaves and flowers. Keep beds and borders free of weeds. Treat corms with Ortho® Malathion Plus® Insect Spray Concentrate before storing. Discard brown, corky corms.

Whiteflies

Whiteflies on underside of ageratum leaf.

Close-up of whitefly larvae.

Problem: Tiny, white, winged insects, ¹⁄₁₆ inch long, feed mainly on the undersides of leaves. Nonflying, scalelike larvae covered with white, waxy powder may also be present on the undersides of leaves. When the plant is touched, insects flutter rapidly around it. Leaves may be mottled and yellow. The plant may grow poorly.

Plants: A wide variety of flowering plants, especially floss flower *(Ageratum)*, coleus, and lantana.

Analysis: The greenhouse whitefly *(Trialeurodes vaporariorum)* is a common insect pest of many garden and greenhouse plants. The four-winged adult lays eggs on the undersides of leaves. The larvae remain attached to the leaves for about a month before changing to the adult form. Both larval and adult forms suck sap from the leaves. The larvae are more damaging because they feed more heavily. Whiteflies excrete a fluid called honeydew, which coats the leaves. A sooty mold fungus may develop on the honeydew, causing leaves to appear black and dirty. In warm-winter areas, insects can be active year-round. The whitefly is unable to live through freezing winters. Spring reinfestations in freezing-winter areas come from migrating whiteflies and from infested greenhouse-grown plants.

Solution: Control whiteflies by spraying with Ortho® Bug-B-Gon® Multi-Purpose Insect Killer Ready-Spray®, Ortho® Systemic Insect Killer, or Ortho® Malathion Plus® Insect Spray Concentrate every 7–10 days as necessary. Spray the foliage thoroughly, being sure to cover both the upper and lower surfaces of the leaves. Whiteflies may also be partially controlled with yellow sticky traps. Eliminating weed hosts in and around the garden will help reduce whitefly populations.

DISCOLORED OR SPOTTED LEAVES: VIRUS
Viruses

Mosaic virus on dahlia leaf.

Mosaic virus on chrysanthemum.

Problem: Leaves may be mottled yellow-green or may be uniformly yellowing. In some cases, the foliage develops yellow rings or the veins may turn yellow. Flowers and leaves may be smaller than normal and distorted. The flowers may be streaked or blotched with light or dark colors, or coloring may be uneven. The plant is usually stunted, and flowering is generally poor. Leaves may be thickened, curled, or distorted. On gladiolus, often the plant blooms prematurely, and the flowers open only partially and then fade rapidly.

Plants: Many annuals, perennials, biennials, and bulbs, especially chrysanthemum, cymbidium orchid, dahlia, carnation and pinks (*Dianthus*), purple coneflower (*Echinacea*), gladiolus, lily, ranunculus, and tulip.

Analysis: Viruses are ultramicroscopic particles capable of invading plant tissue and reproducing in it, usually at the expense of the host plants. They are much smaller than fungi or bacteria and don't have cell walls. Several different plant viruses infect flowering plants, including mosaics, yellows, and ring spots. Mosaic viruses cause the foliage to become mottled or streaked. They are primarily transmitted from plant to plant by aphids. They can also be transmitted from many weeds and ornamental plants. Some plants may be infected with mosaic virus without showing the typical symptoms. Ring-spot viruses cause pale rings to form on the leaves, and stunt viruses cause stunting of plant foliage. Often the symptoms of several viruses overlap. The severity of viral infections depends on the plant and on the strain of virus. In some cases, symptoms of infection may not show up unless several viruses are present in the plant at the same time. Most viruses only slightly impair the growth of the plant and manifest symptoms only under certain conditions. Viral infections do not generally kill the plant but may greatly reduce its overall vigor and beauty. Many viruses are spread by aphids, leafhoppers, and certain other insects and nematodes that feed on diseased plants and transfer the virus to healthy plants. Viral particles can also be transmitted when diseased stock is propagated by cuttings or grafting. If diseased plants are touched or pruned, viruses can be transferred to healthy plants on hands and equipment contaminated by plant sap. *(continued on next page)*

Viruses *(continued)*

Virus color break on tulip flowers.

Virus-damaged gladiolus.

Viruses usually persist in the plant indefinitely. They remain in infected corms and bulbs year after year, so successive plantings of diseased bulbs will produce only poor-quality flowers and foliage. It is best to purchase healthy plants and seeds from a reputable nursery and to discard seeds and cuttings from diseased plants.

Solution: Infected plants can't be cured, but you can reduce the chances of viruses spreading to other plants. Infected plants should be immediately removed and destroyed. Since some viral diseases are readily transmitted by hands and equipment, wash your hands and any containers in hot, soapy water, and disinfect pruning shears after working on infected plants. Purchase only healthy plants. Keep the aphid and leafhopper populations under control. Spray insect-infested plants in the area with Ortho® Systemic Insect Killer, Ortho® Bug-B-Gon® Garden & Landscape Insect Killer, or an insecticide containing malathion. Repeat the spray as often as necessary to keep the insects under control. To reduce the numbers of plants that may harbor viruses, keep your garden free of weeds. Two of the viruses that infect gladiolus are common on vegetables in the bean family; avoid planting gladiolus near beans, clover, cucumbers, squash, melons, and tomatoes. The once-famous showy Rembrandt tulips, which had bizarrely striped or streaked flowers, owed their variegation to viruses. These tulips are no longer available (they are illegal). The striping and streaking found in look-alike modern tulip cultivars is genetic in origin and can't be transferred to other tulips.

LEAVES AND FLOWERS CHEWED
Beetles

Spotted cucumber beetle feeding injury.

Cucumber beetle damage on zinnia.

Problem: Insects chewing holes in the leaves and flowers have hard wing covers folded across their backs, meeting in a straight line down the center. They are frequently brightly colored and shiny.

Plants: A wide variety of annuals, perennials, biennials, and bulbs.

Analysis: Many different species of beetles infest flowers. Two of the most destructive flower pests are Japanese beetles (see page 82) and spotted cucumber beetles, which are yellow-green with black spots. Spotted cucumber beetles are especially attracted to light-colored, late-summer flowers such as tickseed (Coreopsis) and sunflower. In the spring or summer, beetles fly to garden plants and feed on flowers, buds, and leaves. Punctured flower buds usually fail to open, and fully open flowers are often eaten. Because many beetles feed at night, only their damage may be noticed, not the insects. Female beetles lay their eggs in the soil or in flowers in late summer or fall. Emerging larvae crawl down into the soil to spend the winter, or they mature and pass the winter in plant debris. The larvae of some beetles feed on plant roots before maturing in the fall or spring.

Solution: Spray infested plants with Ortho® Systemic Insect Killer, Ortho® Malathion Plus® Insect Spray Concentrate, or Ortho® Bug-B-Gon® Multi-Purpose Insect Killer Ready-Spray®. Make sure that your plant is listed on the product label. Repeat the spray when plants are reinfested, allowing at least 7 days between applications. Avoid spraying when bees are present because bees are also sensitive to the spray. To kill the larvae of spotted cucumber beetles, thoroughly cultivate the soil as soon as temperatures reach 70°F in the spring. Reduce the number of hibernating beetles by cleaning up weeds in the fall.

Caterpillars

Noctuid caterpillar feeding on flower.

Geranium budworm and damage.

Problem: Holes of various sizes and shapes appear in the leaves and buds. Some of the leaves, buds, and flowers may be entirely sheared off. Caterpillars may be seen feeding on flowers and foliage, sometimes only at night. Masses of greenish-brown or black pellets (caterpillar excrement) may be found when the outer leaves are parted.

Plants: A wide variety of annuals, perennials, biennials, and bulbs.

Analysis: Caterpillars, which include cutworms, are smooth, spiny, or hairy, soft-bodied worms with three pairs of prolegs (false legs) near their heads and several pairs of prolegs in the middle and rear of the abdomen. Many species of these moth or butterfly larvae feed on garden plants, usually preferring tissue that is soft and succulent (new growth). The moths and butterflies don't feed on tissue or harm plants, but drink nectar from flowers. Usually the adult moths or butterflies begin laying eggs on garden plants with the onset of warm spring weather. The larvae that emerge from these eggs feed on the leaves, flowers, and buds for 2–6 weeks, depending on weather conditions and species. Caterpillars can go through as many as 11 stages of development. During the first stage, caterpillars may feed as leafminers (between the upper and lower surfaces of leaves) or as skeletonizers (eating only the leaf surface). As the caterpillars increase in size, they require more food, devouring entire leaves. Caterpillar populations fluctuate greatly from year to year because of environmental conditions and natural enemies such as birds, rodents, disease, and other insects. Some caterpillar species have only one generation per year. Other species have numerous generations, so caterpillars of various sizes may be present throughout the growing season. The last generation of caterpillars in the fall survives the winter as pupae in cocoons either buried in the soil or attached to leaves, tree bark, or buildings. Caterpillars that are often seen on flowers include tobacco budworm, corn earworm, cabbage loopers, and cutworms. The first two are closely related larval stages of night-flying moths. Both are striped green, brown, or yellow and range in size from ½–2 inches long. In cooler areas of the country, the caterpillars are present from early spring

Cabbage loopers on calendula.

Corn earworm on ageratum.

to the first frost. In warmer areas, the feeding caterpillars are present year-round. Cabbage loopers are the green larvae of brownish adult moths. These green caterpillars can be up to 1½ inches long and have faint white stripes. Looper damage can occur from early spring through late fall. Cutworms hide in the soil during the day and feed only at night *(see page 85 for more information on cutworms).*

Solution: Inspect flowers periodically for signs of caterpillar infestation. Small numbers of caterpillars may be removed by hand, especially if they are large and easy to see. Spray heavily infested plants with Ortho® Rose & Flower Insect Killer, Ortho® Malathion Plus® Insect Spray Concentrate, Ortho® Systemic Insect Killer, or with the bacterial insecticide *Bacillus thuringiensis* (Bt). Bt is a biological insecticide that paralyzes and destroys the stomach cells of insects that consume it. It is most effective when sprayed on young caterpillars. Repeat treatments at weekly intervals if the plants become reinfested. Make sure that your plant is listed on the product label before using any insecticide, and avoid spraying when bees are present. In the fall, remove plant debris and weeds that may harbor pupae. Deep cultivation of the soil in the fall and early spring will help destroy some of the overwintering pupae.

Japanese beetles

Zinnia damaged by Japanese beetle.

Japanese beetle on rose.

Problem: Leaf tissue has been eaten between the veins, making leaves appear lacy. Flowers are eaten. Winged metallic green-and-bronze beetles, ½ inch long, feed in clusters on the flowers and foliage.

Plants: A wide variety of annuals, perennials, biennials, and bulbs.

Analysis: As its name suggests, the Japanese beetle *(Popillia japonica)* is native to Japan. It was first seen in New Jersey in 1916 and has since become a major pest in the eastern United States. It feeds on hundreds of different species of plants. The adult beetles are present from June to October. They feed only in the daytime and are most active on warm, sunny days. The female beetles live for 30–45 days. Just before they die, they lay their eggs directly under the soil surface in lawns. The grayish-white grubs that hatch from these eggs feed on grass roots. As the weather turns cold in the late fall, the grubs burrow 8–10 inches into the soil, where they hibernate. When the soil warms up in the spring, the grubs migrate back to the surface and resume feeding. They pupate and, in late May or June, reemerge as adult beetles.

Solution: Adult beetles can be controlled with Ortho® Rose & Flower Insect Killer, Ortho® Bug-B-Gon® Garden & Landscape Insect Killer, or Ortho® Systemic Insect Killer. Controls may have to be repeated, because new beetles continue to emerge for about 6 weeks. To better time insecticide applications, use Ortho® Bug-B-Gon® Full-Season Japanese Beetle Traps to monitor the emergence of adult beetles. Before spraying, make sure your plant is listed on the label.

Snails and slugs

Snails feeding on hosta leaves.

Close-up of garden slug.

Problem: Holes are chewed in the leaves or entire leaves may be sheared from the stems. Flowers are partially eaten. Silvery trails wind around on the plants and soil nearby. Snails or slugs may be seen moving around or feeding on the plants, especially at night. Check for them by inspecting the garden at night by flashlight.

Plants: A wide variety of annuals, perennials, biennials, and bulbs, especially delphinium and hosta.

Analysis: Snails and slugs are mollusks and are related to clams, oysters, and other shellfish. They feed on a wide variety of garden plants. Like other mollusks, snails and slugs need to be moist all the time. For this reason, they avoid direct sun and dry places and hide during the day in damp places, such as under flowerpots or in thick ground covers. They emerge at night or on cloudy days to feed. Snails and slugs are similar in appearance except that the snail has a hard shell into which it withdraws when disturbed. Slugs lay white eggs encased in a slimy mass in protected places. Snails bury their eggs in the soil, also in a slimy mass. The young look like miniature versions of their parents.

Solution: Scatter Ortho® Bug-Geta® Snail & Slug Killer in bands around the areas you wish to protect. Also scatter the bait in areas where snails or slugs might be hiding, such as in dense ground covers, weedy areas, compost piles, and flower pot storage areas. Before spreading the bait, wet down the treated areas to encourage snail and slug activity at night. Repeat the application every 2 weeks for as long as snails and slugs are active. Handpicking and disposing of snails and slugs consistently over a long period will greatly reduce populations.

SEEDLINGS DIE
Animal pests

Seedlings eaten by mice.

Pocket gopher mound.

Problem: Plants and seedlings may be partially or entirely eaten. Mounds of soil, ridges, or tunnels may be clustered in the yard. There may be tiny holes in the soil and small, dry, rectangular, brown pellets on the ground near the damaged plants. Various birds and animals may be seen feeding in the garden, or their tracks may be around the damaged plants.

Plants: All annuals, perennials, biennials, and bulbs may be affected.

Analysis: Several different animals feed on flowers. Pocket gophers (found primarily in the West), field mice, rabbits, and deer cause major damage by eating seedlings or mature plants. Certain species of birds feed on seedlings. Moles, squirrels, woodchucks, and raccoons are generally less damaging but may also feed on flower roots, bulbs, and seeds. Even if animals are not directly observed, their burrows, droppings, and tracks are evident.

Solution: Fences, cages or screens, traps, repellents, or baits will protect most garden plants from animal damage or at least greatly reduce the damage. When animal pests need to be removed, traps are usually more effective than poisons, although in some cases poison baits work well. Traps let you see that you have caught the animal, for one thing. If you don't want to kill the animal, you can catch it in a live trap and release it in a nearby wilderness area. Local regulations may govern this. Keep mice out of the garden by surrounding the area with a woven wire fence (¼-inch mesh) at least 12 inches high and buried 12 inches below the soil surface. Gophers and moles are best controlled by trapping. The best way to keep rabbits out of a garden is to enclose it with a fence. Dried blood meal sprinkled near plants may repel rabbits, but it must be reapplied every few days during wet weather. There are many repellents and deterrents developed for deer, but the best way to keep them away from your plants is to erect an 8-foot-tall fence.

Cutworms

Cutworm damage to petunia seedlings.

Surface cutworm.

Problem: Seedlings are chewed or cut off near the ground. Gray, brown, or black worms, 1½–2 inches long, may be found about 2 inches deep in the soil near the base of the damaged plants. The worms curl up into a C-shape coil when disturbed.

Plants: A wide variety of flowering plants, especially annuals.

Analysis: Several species of cutworms attack plants in the flower garden. The most likely pests of seedlings planted early in the season are the surface-feeding cutworms. A single surface-feeding cutworm can sever the stems of many young plants in one night. Cutworms hide in the soil during the day and feed only at night. Adult cutworms are dark, night-flying moths with bands or stripes on their forewings. In the South, cutworms may also attack fall-planted seedlings.

Solution: Apply Ortho® Bug-Geta® Plus Snail, Slug & Insect Killer around the base of undamaged plants when stem cutting is observed. Because cutworms are difficult to control, applications may need to be repeated at weekly intervals. Before transplanting in the same area, apply a preventive treatment of the above product and work it into the soil. Cultivate the soil thoroughly in late summer and fall to expose and destroy eggs, larvae, and pupae. Further reduce damage with cutworm collars around the stem of each plant. Cutworm collars should be at least 2 inches high and surround the plant stem fairly closely. Press them into the soil. Make them out of stiff paper or aluminum foil bent into a cylinder or out of tin cans or paper cups with the bottoms removed.

Germination problems

Damping-off of petunia seedlings.

Damping-off of snapdragon seedlings.

Problem: Seedlings fail to emerge.

Plants: Any flowering plants started from seed.

Analysis: 1. Dehydration: Once the seeds have started to grow, even before they have emerged from the soil, they will die easily if allowed to dry out.
2. Damping-off: Germinating seedlings are very susceptible to damping-off, a plant disease caused by fungi. These fungi inhabit most soils, decaying the young seedlings as they emerge from the seed. Damping-off is favored by wet, cool soil.
3. Slow germination: Seeds of different kinds of plants vary considerably in the amount of time they require to germinate.

4. Poor seed viability: Seeds that are old, diseased, or of inferior quality may fail to germinate.
5. Wrong planting depth: Seeds vary in their planting depth requirements. If planted too deeply or shallowly, the seeds may fail to germinate.
6. Seeds washed away: If a seedbed is watered with a forceful spray or heavy rain, seeds may wash away.
7. Cold weather: Cold weather may delay seed germination considerably or prevent germination entirely.

Solution: 1. Do not allow the soil to dry out completely. Check the seedbed and seed flats at least once a day. Water when the soil surface starts to dry slightly.
2. Allow the soil surface to dry slightly between waterings. Start seeds in Scotts® Potting Soil for Seed Starting. Add Miracle-Gro® Plant Food after the seedlings have produced their first true leaves. Delay planting in spring until the soil warms. Use seed treated with a registered fungicide.
3. Check the instructions on the seed packet to see if your seeds germinate slowly.

4. Purchase seeds from a reputable nursery or seed company. Plant seeds packed for the current year.
5. Plant seeds at the proper depth. Follow the instructions on the commercial seed packet or consult a reputable nursery.
6. Water seedbeds gently. Don't allow the water to puddle and run off. Use a watering can or nozzle that delivers a gentle spray.
7. Even though germination may be delayed, many of the seeds will probably sprout when the weather warms up. The following year, plant seeds later in the season, after the soil has warmed.

Snails and slugs

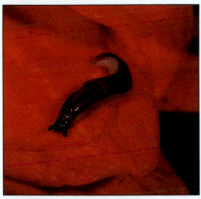

Slug feeding on dahlia flower petal.

Seedlings sheared off by snails.

Problem: Seedlings are sheared off and eaten, with only the stems emerging from the ground. Silvery trails wind around on the plants and soil nearby. Snails or slugs may be seen moving around or feeding on the plants, especially at night. Confirm their presence by inspecting the garden after dark with a flashlight.

Plants: Any flowering plants started from seed.

Analysis: Snails and slugs are mollusks and are related to clams, oysters, and other shellfish. They feed on a wide variety of garden plants. Like other mollusks, snails and slugs need to be moist all the time. For this reason, they avoid direct sun and dry places and hide during the day in damp places, such as under flowerpots or in thick ground covers. They emerge at night or on cloudy days to feed. Snails and slugs are similar in appearance, except that the snail has a hard shell into which it withdraws when disturbed. Slugs lay white eggs encased in a slimy mass in protected places. Snails bury their eggs in the soil, also in a slimy mass. The young look like miniature versions of their parents.

Solution: Apply Ortho® Bug-Geta® Snail & Slug Killer in bands around the areas you wish to protect. Use the bait in areas where snails or slugs might be hiding, such as in dense ground covers, weedy areas, compost piles, or flowerpot storage areas. Before applying the bait, wet down the treated areas to encourage snail and slug activity that night. Repeat the application every 2 weeks for as long as snails and slugs are active in the garden.

Wilted seedlings

Damping-off of marigold seedlings.

Larkspur seedlings suffering from dehydration.

Problem: Seedlings die soon after emerging from the soil and are found shriveled and lying on the soil surface.

Plants: Any flowering plants started from seed.

Analysis: Seedlings may wilt and die from lack of water or from disease.
1. Dehydration: Seedlings are succulent and have shallow roots. If the soil dries out even an inch or so below the surface, seedlings may die.
2. Damping-off: Young seedlings are very susceptible to damping-off, a plant disease caused by fungi. Damping-off is more frequent in wet soil with a high nitrogen level. Damping-off can be a problem when the weather remains cold or cloudy and wet while seeds are germinating or if seedlings are too heavily shaded.

Solution: The numbered solutions below correspond to the numbered items in the analysis above.
1. Do not allow the soil to dry out completely. Water when the soil surface starts to dry slightly. During warm or windy weather, you may need to water several times a day.
2. Allow the soil surface to dry slightly between waterings. Start seeds in Scotts® Starter Fertilizer. Add Miracle-Gro® Plant Food after the seedlings have produced their first true leaves. Protect seeds during germination by coating them with a fungicide containing captan or thiram. Add a pinch of fungicide to a packet of seeds (or ½ teaspoon per pound), and shake well to coat the seeds with the fungicide. Incorporate sand or perlite into the soil mix to increase drainage. Don't add fertilizers that are high in nitrogen until seedlings have produced at least one pair of true leaves. Encourage rapid growth by planting seeds in soil that is the proper temperature for rapid germination. Provide seedlings with bright light and good air circulation.

PROBLEMS ON BULBS, CORMS, & TUBERS
Narcissus bulb flies

Narcissus bulb fly larvae and damage.

Narcissus bulb fly adult.

Problem: Narcissus and daffodil bulbs feel soft and spongy and produce little or no growth after they are planted. Foliage that does emerge is yellow, stunted, and looks grassy. No flowers are produced. In the spring, when daffodils start to bloom, flying insects that resemble small bumblebees (½–¾ inch long) hover around the plants. These black, hairy insects have bands of yellow, buff, or orange around their bodies.

Plants: Narcissus and other bulbs.

Analysis: Narcissus bulb fly *(Merodon equestris)* is a member of the fly family that occasionally attacks other flower bulbs. In the spring, the adult fly lays its eggs on the leaf bases and soil immediately surrounding the plant. The emerging larvae tunnel through the soil to the bulb and feed on the bulb tissue throughout the summer, making it soft and pulpy. The larvae spend the winter in the bulb as wrinkled, plump, grayish-white to yellow maggots ½–¾ inch long. In the spring, they either remain in the bulb or move out into the surrounding soil to pupate. After 1–2½ months, the adult bulb fly emerges and starts the egg-laying cycle again.

Solution: Check all bulbs carefully before planting. If they are soft or spongy, discard them. In May, drench the foliage and surrounding soil with an insecticide containing trichlorfon to kill the adults and emerging larvae. Make sure that daffodils are listed on the insecticide label.

Neck and corm rot

Neck rot on gladiolus.

Penicillium corm rot on gladiolus.

Problem: Foliage may be sparse and turns yellow and dies prematurely. Leaf bases are rotted and may be shredded. Dark reddish-brown to black sunken lesions occur on the corms. Lesions are dry and corky. Black fungal pellets the size of pepper grains may cover the decayed leaf bases and husks of the corms with neck rot. They may enlarge and join, destroying the entire corm. With corm rot, the rotted areas of the corm become covered with a blue-green mold in cool, moist conditions, and the corms are rotted and moldy.

Plants: Gladiolus.

Analysis: Both diseases are caused by fungi. Neck rot fungi attack corms either in storage or in the ground; corm rot fungi infest corms through wounds that occur when the corm is dug out of the ground to be put into storage. The latter problem rarely occurs when corms are properly cured after harvest. After the initial infection from both fungi, the decay spreads up the leaf bases and stem tissue, killing the leaves prematurely. Corms that are planted in cold, wet soil or stored in moist conditions are most susceptible to neck rot. The fungus is spread by contaminated soil and corms. The tiny black fungal pellets that form on infected tissue can survive for 10 years or more in the soil. Corm rot-infected corms rot rapidly when they are stored in warm, humid conditions. The fungus forms masses of blue-green spores and tiny brown fungal pellets that can survive dry conditions and extremes of temperatures to invade healthy corms. If mildly infected corms are planted, they may or may not produce foliage, depending on the severity of the infection.

Solution: Dig corms carefully only after gladiolus leaves have turned entirely yellow. Destroy all corms showing symptoms of either disease. Handle healthy-looking corms carefully to prevent injuries. Dry and cure corms for a week at 85–90°F immediately after digging. Dip them in a fungicide solution containing captan before storing and again before planting. Store cured corms in a dry, cool (40–45°F) location.

Root and bulb rot

Fusarium bulb rot on narcissus.

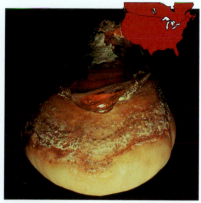

Bulb rot on tulip.

Problem: Plants are stunted and wilting, and the leaves turn yellow or brown. The tips of the lower leaves may be dying and brown, and dead patches may appear along leaf edges. Flower buds may wither and fail to open. The bulbs and roots are sparse and rotted. Bulbs in storage develop a dark, spongy decay that is especially noticeable when the outer fleshy bulb scales are pulled away. White to pink fungal strands may grow in the bulbs. Reddish-brown to black pinhead-size pellets may be on the bulb husks and leaf bases and in the soil immediately surrounding the plant.

Plants: All bulbs, especially lily, tulip, and daffodil (*Narcissus*).

Analysis: Various fungi cause root and bulb rots. They attack and decay the bulbs and roots, causing stunting, wilting, and eventually death of the foliage and flowers. These organisms live in soil and stored bulbs and favor wet soil. Sometimes bulbs in storage are lightly infected, but the fungal decay hasn't progressed far enough to be easily noticed. When planted, these bulbs may rot so quickly that they produce no foliage.

Solution: Remove and destroy infected plants and the soil immediately surrounding them. Check and discard infected bulbs before planting. Avoid wounding bulbs when cultivating around them or handling them. Plant in well-drained soil. Do not replant healthy bulbs in an area where diseased plants have previously grown. Store bulbs in a cool, dry location and check them regularly while in storage.

Scab

Scab on gladiolus corm.

Scab on gladiolus foliage.

Problem: Sunken brown to black lesions on the corm (the "bulb" of the gladiolus plant) are covered with a shiny, varnishlike material and are encircled by raised, brittle rims. Later in the season, after the corms have been planted, many tiny, raised, reddish-brown specks develop on the bases of the emerging leaves. These specks become soft, elongated dead spots. In wet weather these spots may be covered with and surrounded by a shiny, oozing material. The leaves usually fall over.

Plants: Gladiolus.

Analysis: Scab, a disease caused by bacteria *(Pseudomonas marginata),* earns its name from the scablike lesions it produces on the gladiolus corms. The bacteria penetrate the corm tissue, usually where the corm has been injured by soil insects or bulb mites, and then move up into the stem base, producing a soft, watery rot. This decay causes the leaves to fall over. The shiny, varnishlike spots that form on the leaves and corms contain millions of bacteria. Wet, heavy soil and warm temperatures favor the rapid development of this disease. The bacteria can live for several years in infected corms and plant debris. The bacteria usually spread by insects, but they may also be spread by splashing water and by contaminated corms, soil, and tools. Severely infected plants may die.

Solution: No chemical controls this disease. Destroy infected corms. Remove and destroy infected plants. Plant healthy corms in well-drained soil where diseased gladiolus haven't previously grown. Control soil insects to prevent damage to corms.

Tuber rot

Tuber rot on dahlia.

Dahlia plant with healthy foliage and blooms.

Problem: Tuberous roots in storage develop dark brown, sunken areas that are usually dry and firm but are sometimes soft and mushy. Tufts of pink and yellow mold may cover part or all of the roots. Tuberous roots that have been planted may not produce any foliage. If they do, the foliage turns yellow and wilts. When dug up, the roots are rotted and moldy.

Plants: Dahlia.

Analysis: Tuber rot is a plant disease caused primarily by two common soil-inhabiting fungi (*Fusarium* and *Botrytis* spp.). The fungi generally don't infect the tuberous roots unless the roots are wounded. If the roots are damaged when they are dug out of the ground, the fungi will penetrate the wounds and rot the tissue. The roots rot rapidly when they are stored in warm, humid conditions. If tuberous roots suffer frost damage while they are in storage, they will also be susceptible to fungal invasion. Sometimes tuberous roots in storage are contaminated, but the fungal decay has not progressed far enough to be noticed. When they are planted the following spring, they may not produce foliage. If they do produce foliage, the fungus causes wilting, yellowing, and eventually death of the plant.

Solution: Infected roots can't be saved. To prevent tuber rot the following year, dig up the roots carefully after they have matured. Discard any roots that show decay. Handle them carefully to prevent injuries. Store the roots in peat moss in a cool, dark place that is safe from frost.

INDEX

METRIC CONVERSIONS

U.S. Units to Metric Equivalents			Metric Units to U.S. Equivalents		
To Convert	**Multiply By**	**To Get**	**To Convert**	**Multiply By**	**To Get**
Inches	25.4	Millimeters	Millimeters	0.0394	Inches
Inches	2.54	Centimeters	Centimeters	0.3937	Inches
Feet	30.48	Centimeters	Centimeters	0.0328	Feet
Feet	0.3048	Meters	Meters	3.2808	Feet
Yards	0.9144	Meters	Meters	1.0936	Yards

To convert from degrees Fahrenheit (F) to degrees Celsius (C), first subtract 32, then multiply by ⁵⁄₉.

To convert from degrees Celsius to degrees Fahrenheit, multiply by ⁹⁄₅, then add 32.

Take Them Outdoors!

WATERPROOF BOOKS

- Pocket-Sized
- Cleanable
- Durable
- Tear-Resistant
- Lightweight

All Your Garden Tools Should Be This Rugged.